ROADSIDE GIANTS

D1601241

ROADSIDE GIANTS

Brian
and
Sarah
Butko

STACKPOLE
BOOKS

Published by
STACKPOLE BOOKS
5067 Ritter Road
Mechanicsburg, PA 17055
www.stackpolebooks.com

Printed in China

10 9 8 7 6 5 4 3 2 1

FIRST EDITION

Design by Beth Oberholtzer
Cover design by Caroline Stover
Photos by the authors unless otherwise noted

Front Cover (clockwise from left): Randy's Donuts, Los Angeles (*Rick Sebak*); Paul Bunyan, Bemidji, Minnesota (*Bemidji Visitors and Convention Bureau*); Santa Claus at Santa's Lodge, Santa Claus, Indiana; Brooks Catsup Bottle, Collinsville, Illinois; flying saucer gas station, formerly in Ashtabula, Ohio (*Kevin and Lori Butko*); Apatosaurus at Dinosaurland, White Post, Virginia (*Kyle Weaver*); The Gemini Giant at the Launching Pad Café, Wilmington, Illinois; Coney Island, Aspen Park, Colorado; Lucy the Elephant, Margate, New Jersey (*Kyle Weaver*)

Frontispiece: The thirty-five-foot-long lobster at Treasure Village in Islamorada, Florida, intimidates Katrina Prentice of WQED-TV (*Rick Sebak*)

Above: Matchbook for Koffee Kettle, Elizabeth, New Jersey

Back cover: Cowboy Muffler Man at Cowtown Rodeo in Pilesgrove, New Jersey (*Kyle Weaver*)

Library of Congress Cataloging-in-Publication Data

Butko, Brian.
    Roadside giants / Brian and Sarah Butko.– 1st ed.
      p.   cm.
    ISBN-13: 978-0-8117-3228-4 (pbk.)
    ISBN-10: 0-8117-3228-2 (pbk.)
    1. United States–Description and travel.   2. United States–History, Local.
3. Roadside architecture–United States.   4. Mimetic architecture–United States.
5. Historic buildings–United States.   6. Commercial buildings–United States.
I. Butko, Sarah. II. Title.
E169.Z83.B88   2005
306′.0973′090511–dc22

                                            2005009366

CONTENTS

Roadside artist Chuck Biddle visits the Indian in the backyard of Fort Cody Trading Post, North Platte, Nebraska. The giant began life as a regular Muffler Man.

LOOMING OVER THE LANDSCAPE
An Introduction to Roadside Giants

In our family, the best part of a road trip is not stumbling upon a roadside giant, though that's a special occasion too. No, our favorite times are when we set out in search of a giant. As we get near, we dig out our wrinkled directions, though they're often so vague that we're not sure of the exact location. Notes such as "south of Exit 238" leave lots of room for error and could mean failure of the mission: "Nothing towering above the tree line. Look forward and back. Are we even close? The anticipation is killing us! Ahhh, up around the bend, there it is! How could we ever have worried?"

When we began writing *Roadside Giants*, we thought we'd aim it at kids; what better way to inspire the next generation to patronize and care for these places? But we came to realize that few kids would be rushing out to buy or borrow this book. It's adults who like this stuff and pass that appreciation on to their children and grandchildren.

We knew from our own experience that a guidebook was needed. Lots of wonderful resources are available—books we've been reading for twenty-five years and now websites—but as regular travelers, we've often found that not enough information is provided, or it's spread among too many sources. We were also amazed at how much contradictory information we found. Most of all, we wanted to reach the audience beyond hardcore road enthusiasts. Lots of people talk about their wacky vacation memories, and giants are a popular visual prop in movies, yet awareness and appreciation seem to be found only among a fringe audience. It's still often difficult for the public, let alone some historians and civic planners, to recognize such attractions as historic, attractive, and a boon to their local economy.

The roadside giants in this book can be any type of oversize attraction: larger-than-life people, water towers disguised as coffeepots, buildings shaped like fish or shoes. We do not include traditional statues, but we do include dinosaurs and ships that are probably no bigger than what they're modeled on. We chose two dozen sites, some famous, some obscure, then we list a number of similar attractions. That makes for perhaps one hundred giants covered in this book, out of the thousands out there, so if you don't see your favorite, don't take it too hard—our goal was to be inspirational, not inclusive.

This sign in Clinton, Iowa, tells everyone that shoes are repaired here.

Coney Island is a popular name for places that sell hot dogs, such as this café in Grand Island, Nebraska.

The story of roadside giants has been told before, and it is pretty obvious: They were built to catch the attention of potential customers with an extraordinary visual trick. Long before the auto age, businesses displayed signs that represented the product or service being offered: an oversize key, tooth, shoe, scissors, or spectacles. You can find survivors in many downtowns, some still advertising a going concern, others abandoned when the business closed or moved to the suburbs.

At Salzman's Shoe & Boot Repair, on Eighth Avenue in Greeley, Colorado, a blue and white shoe hangs above the entrance of a one-story brick building. The sign sports the family name and is outlined in neon. The business dates to 1935, when Russian immigrant John Salzman arrived in Greeley, a town that then had sixteen shoe-repair shops. He had learned English from reading western novels and could appreciate a sign that announced the business without having to spell it out. He opened at the current location in 1941, but with most folks now replacing rather than repairing their shoes, the family worries that the third generation may be the last to run the store.

When cars came to dominate American life, businesses spread to the roadside and built bigger signs. Even a 3-foot-long shoe was too small, and there isn't time to read a lot of words at thirty-five miles an hour. Some entrepreneurs realized that the biggest sign they had was their building. After 1920, they began to create structures that conveyed what they sold, just like big signs had done.

A number of terms have been used in recent years to describe this literalism in advertising. Some have called it "fantasy" or "fantastic" architecture. David Gebhard called it "Programatic" in his introduction to Jim Heimann and Rip Georges's 1980 book, *California Crazy*. (Gebhard preferred spelling the word with one *m*.) "Mimetic" is also used to describe a building that mimics its function.

The Barrel Club served travelers round the clock at 404 Lincoln Highway (U.S. Route 40) at Benicia Road, Vallejo, between San Francisco and Sacramento. Ripley's Believe It or Not called it the largest barrel in the world. *Russell Rein Collection*

Examples are many and varied, from coffeepots to tepees to fish-shaped cafés. Windmills and milk bottles and ships were also favorites. Then there's the whole category of massive statues built next to a business, from cows to bowling pins to friendly mascots.

Giants also were popular at tourist destinations, be they landmarks, natural attractions, or beach resorts. Lucy the Elephant was raised near Atlantic City even before the invention of the auto; Wisconsin Dells, the Black Hills, and Myrtle Beach drew large crowds and featured larger-than-life attractions.

As auto-oriented commercial strips blossomed, the 1930s became an especially fertile time for giants. A few of those built during the Depression were photographed under the direction of Roy Stryker, notably documentations for the Farm Security Administration and Office of War Information. Among the images are the enormous ice cream cartons of Freda Farms in Berlin, Connecticut; a dog-shaped snack counter with a window flipped up from its belly in Willamette Valley, Oregon; and a memorable pig-shaped stand in Harlingen, Texas.

A splendid article in the September 1934 issue of *Fortune*, "The Great American Roadside," featured a candid view of the Freda Farms cartons. It proclaimed that anyone looking for giant tamales, pigs, or owls should go to California to "behold such haywire crowned and seated in its ultimate glory." If California had a massing of roadside giants, Los Angeles was its locus. One of the best known was the Brown Derby, a restaurant dreamed up by a film producer and built in 1926

The Dutch Mill Tobacco Shop is all that remains of the Dutch Mill Cottage Court (now Dutch Mill Mobile Home Park) at 11937 East Colfax Avenue, U.S. Route 40 through Aurora, Colorado. *Photo by Mark Wolfe*

Freda Farms Ice Cream in Berlin, Connecticut, was similar to the then-expanding Howard Johnson's chain, offering grilled foods, fried clams, and thirty-two flavors of ice cream. This photo, and one of its signs, was snapped in October 1939 by Russell Lee of the Farm Security Administration. *Library of Congress*

in the shape of a bowler hat. The warm weather, not to mention the make-believe climate induced by the movie industry, spawned walk-in chili bowls, puppies, oranges, airplanes, ice cream freezers, toads, and teapots. Only a few survive, but they enjoy a greater-than-average notoriety.

The upper Midwest also became a popular habitat for roadside giants. Mythological woodsman Paul Bunyan is the best known, but you'll come upon oversize buffalo, ducks, moose, and fish—lots of big fish. Canada also has numerous giants, everything from Vikings to trappers to flying saucers. Perhaps it's all the open space, or it may be an outgrowth of the region's abundant folklore. As the authors of Nebraska's 1939 WPA guide wrote: "Stories belong on the frontier, where story-telling whiles away lonely hours, solves problems, and projects heroic symbols. In this way folk tales . . . have double value, as fantasy and as history; in extending life they also reflect ways of living."

After World War II, roads became wider and traffic faster. Roadside giants declined in number and upkeep but were not yet dead. Mahlon Haines, the self-

The Brown Derby restaurant, one of the best-known landmarks in Los Angeles, was nearly destroyed in the 1980s as the neighborhood around it, now called Koreatown, boomed. Part of the hat was moved to the second floor of the nearby Brown Derby Plaza.

The Haines Shoe House was built near Hallam, Pennsylvania, overlooking the Lincoln Highway (now PA Route 462). U.S. Route 30 bypass now speeds close by, but there's no easy access.

proclaimed "Shoe Wizard" of some forty shoe stores, had a flair for crazy advertising. Sometimes he would stand up at baseball games and pay anyone who could identify him. A Shoe House was his ultimate gimmick, built in 1948 just east of York, Pennsylvania. He added shoe-themed decorations, and the front door still has a stained-glass window with an image of Haines holding a shoe. He offered the house free to elderly couples for a weekend or to honeymooners who had a Haines shoe store in their town.

Technology brought new materials such as fiberglass, which made molding easier and mass production possible. The best-known application was for Muffler Men, giant people that mostly advertised muffler shops and tire dealers. Many of the other figures from the past couple decades have been made by a Wisconsin firm called Fiberglass Animals, Shapes, and Trademarks (FAST). FAST's work ranges from Big Boys to miniature golf animals to truly giant figures such as the walk-through Muskie at the Freshwater Fishing Hall of Fame and the Jolly Green Giant in Blue Earth, Minnesota. The grounds around the factory are strewn with molds and pieces awaiting a home.

Awareness of roadside architecture surfaced in the 1960s, with the rise of pop art and an interest in public history. Other than Muffler Men, few roadside giants were being built by then, though some businesses still employed giant signs; for Arby's roast beef chain it was a neon hat, with roofs recalling the bow of a covered wagon. Many giants were bulldozed because of a lack of purpose or cheap construction, usually plywood covered in stucco. (In this book and many recollections, concrete and stucco are used interchangeably; stucco is cement mixed with sand.)

Perhaps the turning point of affection for giants resulted from a disdain for one of them. Peter Blake's 1964 book, *God's Own Junkyard*, contrasted pastoral scenes with traffic jams, suburban sprawl, and trash heaps. Roadside clutter was a recurring theme, and sitting serenely on page 102 was Long Island's Big Duck. Back then, the owners were still in the fowl-selling business, with a sign advertising roasted ducks, turkeys, and cornish game hens. The facing page has snapshots

Mandarin and Szechuan cooking are the specialties at The China Clipper, 495 Green-brae Avenue in Sparks, Nevada. The sailing ship opened as Bill's Fish and Chips in 1971 and has also served as Neptune's Galley. *Photo by Carol Ingald*

showing families enjoying ducks at a lake. The inference is obvious: The Duck is unnatural, a blight on the landscape. The book makes a good case in many of its contrasting photos, but some, like the Duck, were open to alternate interpretations, which the author himself later admitted.

A response came from architects Denise Scott Brown and Robert Venturi, who had already been promoting an appreciation of less formal "pop architecture." Inspired rather than offended by Blake's photo of the Duck, they coined the term "duck" to better represent mimetic architecture. Its first mention was not, as is often cited, in their landmark 1972 study, *Learning from Las Vegas* (with Steven Izenour), but was applied four years earlier in a March 1968 essay in *Architectural Forum*, "A Significance for A&P Parking Lots, or Learning from Las Vegas." Half a year later, they also penned "On Ducks and Decoration" for *Architecture Canada*. Scott Brown and Venturi likewise introduced the phrase "decorated shed" to indicate a building that has only one element changed or exaggerated to attract attention, such as the towering arches at period McDonald's.

By the 1970s, artists such as John Baeder and Ralph Goings, as well as photographer John Margolies, raced to capture rapidly disappearing roadside businesses. The Society for Commercial Archeology was formed in 1979, intent on documenting such places. The year 1984 saw the publication of *The Well-Built Elephant* by J. J. C. Andrews and *The Colossus of Roads* by Karal Ann Marling. The former documented in pictures and text a selection of surviving giants. The latter remains one of the few scholarly treatments of the subject, with emphasis on myth and symbolism in the upper Midwest. The decades since have seen the continued destruction of the early auto

Roadside researcher Larry Cultrera says, "In the summer, my wife, Denise, and I always manage to get up to Ipswich, Massachusetts, every few weeks to get some fried clams at the Clam Box." The splayed roof is just like the flaps of a cardboard take-out carton. *Photo by Larry Cultrera*

Mammy's Cupboard, a popular café in Natchez, Mississippi, recalls a time when such caricatures were common in American popular culture. *Photo by Rick Sebak*

landscape, but with interest groups, publications, and websites continually arising, the pace has slowed some.

Communities increasingly embrace roadside giants as a way to celebrate their heritage. It's fairly simple when repainting a water tower to have it communicate the town's claim to fame or exhibit a sense of whimsy, making it resemble a peach, watermelon, golf ball, or hot-air balloon. Oversized statues erected in municipal parks inevitably draw attention—and visitors—to small towns, but the debate can turn heated over paying for upkeep. In areas struggling with an economic downturn, it becomes an issue whether to spruce up the town's roadside giant when local roads, schools, and people need support.

Some of the old giants, such as concrete tepees and American Indian Muffler Men, are now considered improper. Perhaps the most controversial is Mammy's Cupboard, a café inside a black woman with a skirt made of bricks. The 28-foot-tall Mammy was built in 1940 near Natchez, Mississippi, on U.S. Route 61, a major highway to New Orleans. The owner was a hostess for the town's annual tours of antebellum mansions and presumed Mammy would appeal to the same tourists. The Mammy figure was portrayed in the popular film *Gone With the Wind*, released in 1939, about the time plans for the building were underway. No harm may have been intended, but these places undoubtedly reflect a stereotype, and they were built when Native Americans, African Americans, and other minorities were not even welcome at many roadside businesses. That's why these buildings are also interesting historic artifacts, helping us better understand those

Giant genies are tied down and ready for the long haul from Southern California to their new home at the American Sign Museum in Cincinnati. They were donated by Loren Sign and restored by Eric Kilb, president of the Glass Hand, which also makes Big Boy statues for Frisch's restaurants. One of the genies stands at the museum's entrance. *American Sign Museum/Photo by Loren Electric Sign, Montebello, California*

time periods. Mammy's black skin was repainted a lighter tone in the 1960s in reaction to the civil rights movement.

A few buildings are still made like giant things. In recent years, the Longaberger headquarters was designed to look like one of the company's baskets. The Robert Fulton Inn in Lancaster, Pennsylvania, resembles a paddlewheel boat. And many towns have Hard Rock Cafés featuring giant electric guitars, attracting customers just like a big tooth or eyeglasses once did.

Places are still being lost, too. The Twin T-P restaurant (later known as the Twin Tepees) in Seattle was bulldozed in summer 2001 after a fire the previous year closed it. Fire also did in the S.S. Grand View Ship Hotel, east of Bedford, Pennsylvania, that October.

Luckily, increased awareness has helped just as many to be preserved. Hampton Hotels' Save-A-Landmark Program has spent more than $1 million to refurbish nineteen roadside attractions, some of them giants. Two of these sites–the Big Duck and the Blue Whale–are featured in this book. Meanwhile, Randy's Donuts made the cover of *Frommer's Los Angeles 2005*, but it appears nowhere in the text. Like so many giants, it is more window dressing than a legitimate entry.

They may not be fine art, but who cares? Roadside giants are significant as historic buildings and, more important, cultural landmarks. They serve as local gathering spots and come to represent their towns to outsiders. A roadside giant is likely the only reason you've ever heard of some small towns or businesses. They continue to sell and entertain.

The Big Duck
Hampton Bays, New York

The Big Duck has moved around Long Island but now nests at Sears Bellows County Park. *Photo by Rick Sebak*

Martin Maurer and his wife, Jeule, were among the scores of people who sold ducks and duck eggs on Long Island. They tended to some thirty thousand ducks at their farm along West Main Street in the Upper Mills part of Riverhead. On a trip to California, the Maurers visited a café shaped like a coffeepot. Martin came back inspired to build a stand shaped like a giant duck.

George Reeve was hired as a carpenter. Two men Reeve hired got a real duck from Maurer to use as a model and either tied it to their porch or roasted it (accounts differ). They then built a wood frame and covered it with wire and stucco. Ford Model T taillights served as the eyes, which glowed red at night.

The Duck opened on West Main Street in June 1931. Atlas Cement featured the funny-shaped store on their calendar and *Popular Mechanics* profiled the Duck in November 1932.

The Duck served not only as a building, but also as a giant sign, needing no words to announce what was sold inside. In the 1960s, the Duck even became a symbol for such buildings as signs, its name being used as a term for places built to visually represent their purpose.

Long before such heady status, in 1936, the Maurers moved their Big Duck four miles southeast, to Flanders Road (NY Route 24) near Flanders. It was closer to their new farm and, more important, on a well-traveled road. The Duck did well for half a century, but with folks buying fewer ducks and duck eggs every year, it closed in 1984 and in 1987 the land was sold. The giant had to be moved.

Locals loved it and wanted to save it, but what would they do with a homeless duck-shaped building?

STATS

SIZE: 20 feet tall, 30 feet long, 15 feet wide from the tips of its folded wings

MADE OF: Wood framing and wire mesh covered with stucco

BUILT: 1931

The Duck was donated to Suffolk County, which moved it a bit further east on Flanders Road in January 1988. Plans called for gathering other local icons of the road, but this never happened. Instead, Friends for Long Island's Heritage and other supporters raised $30,000 to restore what had become the premier local landmark. The Duck was listed in the National Register of Historic Places. In 1991, model Christie Brinkley recorded a two-minute history of the Duck, which was broadcast to passing drivers.

Ducks are no longer sold at the Big Duck, but you can still go inside and buy duck umbrellas, T-shirts, sweatshirts, and other duck souvenirs. Duckkeeper Barbara "Babs" Bixby entertains visitors with duck puns and a few duck "tails." The little building closes in winter, but not before the annual Big Duck Holiday Lighting Ceremony. The county parks department works with local community associations to trim the Duck with garlands, holly, and hundreds of lights. Duck Carols are sung by schoolchildren on the special night. In 2004, Quacker Jack of the Long Island Ducks made a guest appearance, and then Santa arrived to turn on the decorations.

The Big Duck is still a sign, but instead of indicating what is sold inside, the Duck and many other roadside giants like it increasingly have come to symbolize the heritage of a region and the efforts of newer generations to preserve part of roadside commercial history.

If you visit . . .

The Big Duck is east of Flanders on the eastern end of Long Island. It is in Sears Bellows County Park at 61 Bellows Pond Road, just off Flanders Road (Riverhead–Hampton Bays Road/NY Route 24). Take NY Route 27 (Sunrise Highway, POW/MIA Memorial Highway) to exit 65, then follow Route 24. The Duck is operated by the Friends for Long Island's Heritage and is open daily from April through December.

The theme of the Mother Goose house, north of Hazard, Kentucky, is carried through with eight egg-shaped windows.

If you like the Big Duck, you'll also like . . .

- **The Mother Goose House** on KY Route 476, just north of Hazard, Kentucky. To design this building, George Stacy shot a goose, and his wife cooked it until all that remained was the skeleton. After six years of work, in 1940, they moved in. The goose looks as though it's perched on a nest, and the house has egg-shaped windows. It's 45 feet long, 28 feet wide, and 15 feet high at the head. A grocery and gas station added in front closed long ago, but next door is the Mother Goose Food Mart. The goose has been featured in the *New York Times* and on the *Oprah Winfrey Show*.
  www.state.ky.us/agencies/khc/goose.htm
  http://hazardkentucky.com/more/goose.htm

- **The Big Chicken** in Marietta, Georgia, is a 56-foot-tall steel rooster atop a KFC restaurant on U.S. Route 41 and GA Route 120. It was built in 1963 and restored in 1993. Its eyes roll and the beak moves.

- A 12-foot-tall, 3,000-pound concrete **egg** in Mentone, Indiana (south of Warsaw), celebrates the town's main industry. Built in 1946, it has a state map painted on it. The egg is at the corner of Main Street (IN Route 25) and Morgan Street.

- **The flag-themed egg** in front of the local co-op plant in Winlock, Washington. It honors the town's heritage, which is also showcased in its annual Egg Day festivities. The egg is made of fiberglass over wire mesh. The town wants everyone to know that it's the World's Largest Egg. Though it's the largest, Mentone, Indiana, still claims their concrete egg is the heaviest.

Tail o' the Pup
Los Angeles, California

In his introduction to *California Crazy*, the late architectural historian David Gebhard called the decade from 1925 to 1934 the heyday of California's Programatic building boom. By the time World War II ended, few new roadside giants were being built there, and old ones were already being knocked down. A couple guys had begun planning for one back in 1938, even having an architect design the structure, but before their dream could be realized, they headed off to the war. When they got back, they finally built it: a hot-dog-shaped stand with a serving window that opened into an awning or folded into the structure at night.

Tail o' the Pup opened in 1945 or 1946 (no one seems sure) at 311 North LaCienega, in Los Angeles's Westside neighborhood near North Hollywood. It was squeezed on a street corner, and like the farmhouse in the children's classic *The Little*

STATS
SIZE: 8 feet tall, 17 feet long
MADE OF: Wood covered with wire mesh and stucco
BUILT: 1945

House, it was encroached on by development more each year. By 1985, plans for the Hotel Sofitel threatened the hot dog. Lots of fans spoke out for its preservation, and a new home was found just one block east. A grand reopening featured Jay Leno from *The Tonight Show*.

It has appeared in movies such as the 1984 thriller *Body Double* and was in the first episode of Pamela Anderson's TV series "VIP," titled "It Beats Working at a Hot Dog Stand," in which her character starts the show employed at the Pup. Anderson's picture now hangs there along with other famous fans of the stand.

West Hollywood is home to America's best-known hot dog stand.
Photo by Rick Sebak

Six different kinds of hot dogs are offered, including the Boston Celtic, topped with baked beans, mustard, and onions, and the Mexican Olé, with chili, cheese, and onions. Other toppings include chopped nuts, and hamburgers are available too. You can sit at a table with an umbrella or eat while walking to the nearby Hard Rock Café or Beverly Center Mall.

Tail o' the Pup has been owned since 1975 by Eddie Blake and his son Dennis. An estimated five million hot dogs have crossed its counter over the years. It's surrounded by trendy cafés, but as Dennis says, "Not everybody in L.A. is a vegetarian."

If you visit . . .

Tail o' the Pup is at 329 North San Vicente Boulevard, just north of Beverly Boulevard and Cedars Sinai Medical Center.

If you like the Tail o' the Pup, you'll also like . . .

- **Coney Island**, a hot-dog-in-a-bun-shaped restaurant in Colorado's Aspen Park (or Conifer; this seems to be a location versus postal address issue). The concrete dog is 42 feet long, 15 feet tall, and 14 tons. Once known as Coney Island Dairy Land, it was built in 1965 on Colfax Avenue in Denver, then moved here in 1969. It closed in 1999 and was for sale (1.3 acres for $1 million), but it has been doing fine since under Lisa and Taylor Firman. Small tables in each corner seat ten. A low-priced menu has different dogs plus fries, onion rings, and burgers. It's southwest of Denver at 25877 U.S. Route 285 (actually on parallel Conifer Road, which looks to be old 285) at South Dallman Drive.

- The **hot dog couple** on the roof (since 1948) of Superdawg, a drive-in restaurant at 6363 North Milwaukee Avenue at West Devon Avenue, northwest of downtown Chicago. The 12-foot-tall mascots, looking like Tarzan and Jane, also lord over "superburgers" and "super sundaes."
www.superdawg.com

- The 30-foot-long **chili dog** atop the Waaa Daa Hot Dog Shoppe at 1975 West State Street (U.S. Route 62) in Alliance, Ohio, east of Canton. City officials worried that the rooftop tube steak would make the town look like Las Vegas. The city sued the owner and the Board of Zoning Appeals for approving the

The line usually stretches out the door, and the tables are filled, at Coney Island in Aspen Park, Colorado.

variance that allowed the rooftop sign, but the court ruled in favor of the dog. City officials were indeed prophetic; a month after the dogfight ended, a big burger appeared at a car dealer down the road. This time, a zoning-board member was against it, figuring that if the trend went unchecked, the street would soon resemble "a big food court or something."

• **A Muffler Man holding a hot dog** draws Route 66 tourists to Arch Street between Race and Vine streets in Atlanta, Illinois. Nicknamed Tall Paul because he resembles Paul Bunyan he advertised Bunyon's hot dog shop (hence the frankfurter) in nearby Berwyn starting in 1963. He'd been hit by a car, shot by arrows, even lost an eye in a drive-by shooting, but in December 2003, the owners put him on permanent loan to his new town, which restored him in conjunction with the Illinois Route 66 Association.

• **The Tamale** stand at 6421 Whittier Boulevard, in the Montebello neighborhood of east Los Angeles, built in 1928. It no longer sells food, but its "corn husk wrapper" can still be seen, bunched on each end of the twenty-eight-foot-long tamale, squeezed between two other buildings.

Muffler Men and Uniroyal Gals
Across the United States

If ever there was something that found fame years after it peaked, it's Muffler Men. Even the name itself is a recent creation, coined by the road-hardened experts at Roadside America (see page 89) because so many of them were used by car-repair shops. The friendly fiberglass giants have that website to thank for newfound fame three decades after the last molds were broken.

Fiberglass came to prominence in the 1950s as the material used for Corvette bodies. By the 1960s, it was popular with boat makers and car customizers such as George Barris, who created vehicles for TV and movies. Prewitt Fiberglass of Venice, California, began using the material to make giants for the auto and food industries. According to Steve Dashew, the Muffler Men were almost all derivatives of a woodsman made for the Paul Bunyan Café on Route 66 in Flagstaff, Arizona, just before he bought the company in 1963. Renamed International Fiberglass, the company made thousands of other statuary, too, mostly animals. Business tailed off around the time of the gas crisis, and Dashew closed the company about 1974.

Muffler Men sold for $1,000 to $2,800. The men were between 18 and 25 feet tall. The standard model had a square jaw with just a hint of a grin and wore a short-sleeved shirt well suited for

Westmoreland Tire on U.S. Route 119 North in Greensburg, Pennsylvania, repainted its football man every few years to reflect the fan favorite. A couple years ago it was made number 8, Tommy Maddox, who remains now that the shop has closed.

STATS

SIZE: 18 to 25 feet tall

MADE OF: fiberglass

BUILT: 1962–74

service station use. Different arms, legs, and heads could be mixed and matched. Standard hands had the right palm facing up, left facing down. Dashew said that was a holdover from the original Bunyan's need to hold an axe; there was no need for expensive retooling, especially since so many were to hold a muffler.

The most common surviving variant seems to be a bearded lumberjack, looking just like the original Paul Bunyan. Cowboys are also seen, as are burger-holding cooks. Not so common, but still a factory issue, was a pirate with optional eye patch or peg leg.

An American Indian was also available, usually with the right arm raised in a stereotypical "How" greeting. Other Indians have been converted from regular Muffler Men, such as one behind the Fort Cody Trading Post in North Platte, Nebraska. It was bought for $100 in the late 1960s from a gas station across from the original location; look closely and you'll see a painted-over bow tie.

A "half-wit," or "country bumpkin," as Dashew called it, is a version of the hayseed boy popular in American culture, similar in appearance to Alfred E. Neuman of *Mad Magazine*. Though harder to find, they exist at Ken's Muffler and Brakes in Dallas, Texas; the Bargain Hunterz discount clothing store (wearing blue jeans and Hawaiian shirt) on Atherton Road in Flint, Michigan; and in front of Old Time Photo, Lake Ozark, Missouri.

The company did not ignore feminine pulchritude either. Uniroyal Gals were 18-foot-tall giants sent to U.S. Tire Company stores as a promotional gimmick. The surviving eleven or so ladies reflect 1960s fashions. Some wear bikinis; others, such as the one at the Werbany Tire Town dealership in Gloucester Township, New Jersey, have on skirts.

Being out of production for so long, most of these giants have been remodeled once or twice to fit a new owner's needs. In Wilmington, Illinois, the Gemini Giant (which is under copyright) had the traditional Muffler Man look when it was purchased in 1965 for $3,500; it was remade to advertise

In 2003, a Muffler Man in Ham Lake, Minnesota, was purchased for $10,000, shipped at a cost of $2,000, and remade—an arm had to be flipped—as mascot for the JackHammers, a minor league baseball team at Silver Cross Field in Joliet, Illinois.

This Muffler Man variant is at Pirates miniature golf course on the Boardwalk in Ocean
City, New Jersey. *Photo by Kyle Weaver*

the Launching Pad Café drive-in restaurant on IL Route 53, formerly the celebrated U.S. Route 66. Everyone in
Elizabeth, New Jersey, gives directions
from the Carpet Guy on U.S. Business
Routes 1 and 9. In Greensburg, Pennsylvania, a tire shop made its Muffler
Man into a Pittsburgh Steeler, repainting the number every few years to match
a popular player (with the shop closed,
it's stuck as number 8, for quarterback
Tommy Maddox). On U.S. Route 40 in

Havre de Grace, Maryland, a giant was
dressed in camouflage to honor Desert
Storm soldiers. La Salsa Mexican restaurant in Malibu, California, converted a
soda jerk to a sombrero-wearing waiter,
the bottom of his hamburger bun trans-
formed into a serving tray.

Perhaps the greatest concentration
of Muffler Men is at Lake George,
New York. Magic Forest, an amusement park just south of town, has at
least four: a dark-skinned Pecos Bill, a
clown, a bearded Amish-looking half-
wit holding an axe and wearing a blue

Judy DeMoisy, the "Catsup Bottle Lady,"
who helped save the Brooks Catsup Bottle
in Collinsville, Illinois, visits a Uniroyal
Gal in Peoria, Illinois. *Photo by Mike "Big
Tomato" Gassmann*

This soda jerk Muffler Man helps sell ice cream in Natural Bridge, Virginia. *Photo by Kyle Weaver*

shirt, and a lumberjack. There is also an axe-wielding lumberjack at a nearby minigolf, said to be the Paul Bunyan from the 1964–65 New York World's Fair. The nearby town of Luzerne has a lumberjack that once advertised the Swiss Trail Campground, but now he stands battered, missing an arm and his head, perhaps waiting for fellow Muffler Men to come to his rescue.

If you like these Muffler Men, you'll also like . . .

- **Carpet guy** and a pair of **Muffler Man pants**, at Wilson's Carpet on the north side of U.S. Truck Routes 1 and 9, under the Pulaski Skyway. The carpet-holding guy (actually, it's a roll of sheet metal) was bought from Lafayette Sign in Jersey City, which had gotten him from an Amoco. When Wilson moved here in 1990, the carpet man came along. The mysterious pants behind the business were painted orange-pink just so folks will ask why. The carpet guy gained fame in recent years from a shot in the opening of "The Sopranos" TV series.

- **The hat-wearing half-wit** at Wacky Golf on the upper boardwalk, Seaside Heights, New Jersey. Another on nearby Casino Pier inexplicably wields an axe. More Muffler Men and other giants dominate the area.

Cowboy Sam has welcomed diners to the Cadet restaurant on U.S. Route 422 in Kittanning, Pennsylvania, since 1968 (with a few years out of service after a car hit him). The former drive-in has been under the same ownership since 1951.

- A factory-made, bare-chested **American Indian** at Cherokee Village Auto Sales on WV Route 95 West, a quarter mile west of WV Route 14, south of downtown Parkersburg, West Virginia.

- **The Uniroyal Gals**, still mostly found at tire businesses. Look for the Werbany Tire Town's **Doll** at 1337 Black Horse Pike, Hilltop, New Jersey; **the cheerleader** at Reid Bethel Tire on Business Route 87 in Lamesa, Texas; **the tire gal** at Peoria Plaza Tire Company in Peoria, Illinois; and the now-blonde **gal with sandwich platter** at Martha's Cafe, Blackfoot, Idaho.

- **The Muffler Man**, **Uniroyal Gal**, and **two Big Johns** (made to hold bags for a grocery chain) at Glenn Goode's fiberglass molding and sandblasting business, 1651 f.m. 371/Walnut Bend Road, north of U.S. 82 East, Gainesville, Texas.

- **The Gemini Giant**, spaceman mascot of the Launching Pad Cafe at 810 East Baltimore Street (U.S. Route 53/Historic Route 66) in Wilmington, Illinois. **www.launchingpadrt66.com**

Paisano Pete
Fort Stockton, Texas

In December 2003, Pete the roadrunner had a small party at his new digs. The town mascot had just received an elevated base with trees and irrigated planters. They were part of a larger program by the Texas Department of Transportation to encourage landscaping and economic development efforts around the Permian Basin. The city also offered in-kind work toward the $75,000 project.

Pete has welcomed folks to Fort Stockton since 1980, when then-mayor Gene Cummings thought it would be a nice addition to the town, since the birds are common in the area. A roadrunner was ordered from Creative Displays (now FAST) of Sparta, Wisconsin, at a cost of $6,250. A Name the Roadrunner contest brought twenty-one suggestions. Eric Mayo won the $50 prize, choosing Paisano, Italian for "friend," and Pete for . . . well, probably for alliteration.

STATS

SIZE: 11 feet tall, 22 feet long

MADE OF: fiberglass

BUILT: 1980

Pete's triangle of land has been spruced up over the years, including the addition of flagpoles, but the work in 2003 was the biggest makeover. Pete carries on the tradition of city councils and chambers of commerce everywhere in taking a local symbol of pride and creating a memorable attraction for visitors.

If you visit . . .

Paisano Pete poses with roadside fan Maureen Freark. Photo by Doug Towne

Pete stands frozen in midstride at the intersection of Main Street and Dickinson Boulevard, just off I-10 in western Texas.

If you like Paisano Pete, you'll also like . . .

• **World's Largest Roadrunner** in Las Cruces, New Mexico. Pete is pretty big, but the title of world's largest belongs to this creation, about 15 feet high and maybe 50 feet long. Artist Olin Calk crafted the giant from recycled materials, including old computers, tennis shoes, broken toys, and car parts. It was made at the city dump, but when that closed, the city moved it here. It overlooks the Rio Grande valley from a rest area on the eastbound (south) side of I-10, between mile markers 134 and135, a few miles west of Las Cruces, which is just north of El Paso, Texas, and the southern U.S. border.

Maxie, the World's Largest Goose, is ready to take flight from a community park in Sumner, Missouri. *Photo by Mike Gassman*

- **Claire the Loon** (get it, Claire de Lune?), which sits next to the Mercer, Wisconsin, Chamber of Commerce to honor the "Loon Capital of the World." It can be found on the south end of Mercer, along U.S. Route 51, about ten miles from Michigan's Upper Peninsula.

- **The rattlesnake** that greets visitors to the Freer Chamber of Commerce and honors the town's Rattlesnake Roundup. See it at 154 East TX Route 44, Freer, in southern Texas.

- **The World's Largest Jackalope**, a mythical half jackrabbit, half antelope, that guards the town of Douglas, Wyoming. There's a picture of author James Michener and his wife, Mari, posing by it in the 1978 book *In Search of Centennial*, before it was moved to a park.

- **Maxie the World's Largest Goose**, with a wingspan of 65 feet. Sculpted in 1976 and flown in by helicopter for the annual Goose Festival, she honors Swan Lake National Wildlife Refuge in north-central Missouri. The refuge was established by Congress in 1937 to provide food and water for migratory waterfowl. It was created when the Civilian Conservation Corps turned 10,670 acres of land into wetlands. Maxie is south of U.S. Route 36 on MO Route 139 in Sumner, Missouri, "Wild Goose Capital of the World."

Hat n' Boots
Service Station
Georgetown, Washington

The Hat n' Boots await restoration at their new home in Oxbow Park, Georgetown, Washington. *Photo by Frank Brusca*

The Hat n' Boots was built as part of a gas station called Premium Tex. The trio was to be part of Frontier Village, a western-style shopping center, but a grocery store was the only other element built. The hat sat atop the station's office, while the colorful western boots served as his and hers restrooms. The attraction received patent number 177,189 on March 20, 1956.

In its first three years, the Hat n' Boots sold more gasoline than any other station in Washington. But when I-5 opened, cars began taking the new road instead of the old Pacific Highway (WA Route 99). The station made a brief appearance in the opening credits of *National Lampoon's Vacation* movie, but fame couldn't

STATS	Hat	Boots
SIZE:	44 feet wide	22 feet high
MADE OF:	steel, wire, and concrete	steel, wire, and concrete
BUILT:	1955	1955

pay the bills, and it closed in 1988. For fifteen years, the Hat n' Boots sat empty, the paint fading and weeds growing around the structures. Rumor was that brave skateboarders were climbing the hat to ride its brim.

The Department of Natural Resources, which owned the land the Hat n' Boots was on, didn't mind the buildings being preserved, but officials wanted them moved. Plans were begun in 2001 to build a park where the attraction could be relocated. A vacant lot was chosen on the 6400 block of Corson Avenue South. The Georgetown Community Council obtained title to the structures for $1 and secured grants to fund their removal and restoration.

Park construction started in November 2003 on paths and plantings. It was named Oxbow Park in reference to the historic Duwamish River oxbow, which surrounded Georgetown before the river was redirected in 1917.

Finally, on December 12, 2003, the hat was moved down the street, then the boots. Restoration is on hold while additional funding is secured, but for now, the Hat n' Boots is safe n' sound.

If you visit . . .

The Hat n' Boots have spent their life in Georgetown, south of Seattle. They were first at 6800 Corson Avenue South (WA Route 99, the old Pacific Highway), on the corner of East Marginal Way, but they are now settled into Oxbow Park at 6400 Corson Avenue South, between that road and Carleton Avenue South.

www.hatnboots.org
www.cityofseattle.net/parks/proparks/projects/oxbow.htm

If you like the Hat n' Boots, you'll also like . . .

- The massive **sombrero** covering the roof of El Sombrero restaurant, at 2819 North Nevada Avenue in Colorado Springs, Colorado.

- The approximately 10-foot fiberglass **sneaker** outside a hotel owned by basketball coach Steve Alford in New Castle, Indiana, south of town on IN Route 3. www.ez-look.com/stevealfordinn

- The 52-foot-tall **Tex the Cowboy** at the state fairgrounds immediately east of downtown Dallas. Since 1952, Tex has talked and waved to visitors. Close cousins are the 40-foot-tall **Vegas Vic**, in Las Vegas, since 1946, and 90-foot-tall **Wendover Will**, standing right on the border of northern Utah and Nevada since 1952.

- The 45-foot-tall pile of empty **oil cans** in Casselton, North Dakota. Max Taubert began piling them in 1933 around a windmill to advertise his gas station.

Baseball Bat and Glove
Louisville, Kentucky

It's easy to find the Louisville Slugger headquarters.

The Hillerich & Bradsby Company has been making bats since 1884. That's when eighteen-year-old John "Bud" Hillerich, a woodworker like his dad, saw an opportunity. He already was making bats for himself and friends, so when he saw Louisville player Pete Browning break a bat, Bud offered to carve one just for him, perhaps the first custom bat ever made for a pro player.

STATS	Bat	Glove
SIZE:	120 feet high	12 by 9 feet
MADE OF:	steel	limestone
BUILT:	1995	1998

The company's Louisville Slugger has become standard equipment in major league baseball. When Hillerich & Bradsby wanted to advertise its new headquarters, factory, and the Louisville Slugger Museum, it decided to make a big bat—a very big bat, at 120 feet tall and 34 tons (a real one measures about 34 inches). To do such a big job, the company hired Caldwell Tanks, a builder of water towers such as the giant catsup bottle in Collinsville, Illinois.

Installed in 1995, the Big Bat, tilted 11.5 degrees from vertical, is an exact replica of Babe Ruth's 34-inch Louisville Slugger from the 1920s. It includes a replica signature of Bud Hillerich.

Inside the Louisville Slugger museum is another giant: a 4-foot-high, 17-ton glove. Visitors can crawl on it or through the folded opening. The glove was crafted by Kimberly Hillerich and Albert Nelson from 450-million-year-old Kentucky limestone.

You can tour the factory any day, where bats are made most days except Sundays and holidays, and view videos about how bats are made. After the tour, visitors get souvenir miniature bats to remind them of the real ones, which are two times larger, as well as the giant one that's eighty times larger.

If you visit . . .

Louisville Slugger Museum is in downtown Louisville, 800 West Main Street. A parking garage is adjacent. The bat is outside, leaning against the building. The glove can be seen inside with paid admission.

www.sluggermuseum.org

If you like the Baseball Bat and Glove, you'll also like . . .

- The boiler stack outside Yankee Stadium, at 161st Street and River Avenue in the Bronx, painted to look like **Babe Ruth's baseball bat**. This 120-foot-tall bat features a Louisville Slugger logo and Ruth's signature. Yankee Stadium opened a year after the team purchased Ruth from the Boston Red Sox. Ruth christened the park at its opening on April 18, 1923, in a game with the Red Sox, in which he scored a three-run homer. The Bat is adjacent to Gate 4. The stadium is accessible from I-87/Major Deegan Expressway.

- The **baseball-shaped water tower** on the east side of I-77, just south of Exit 88, in Fort Neill, South Carolina.

- The big **golf ball** south of Newark, Ohio, on OH Route 79.

This golf ball has been repainted but still draws customers to a small shopping plaza southwest of Columbus, Ohio.

- **The World's Largest Hockey Stick and Puck** in Duncan, British Columbia, Canada, made for the 1986 World's Fair Exposition in Vancouver. When the fair ended two years later, a contest was held to find a new home for the stick and puck. Out of more than thirty entrants, the winner was the Cowichan Community Centre in Duncan. Residents and businesses raised $150,000 to prepare the site and dismantle and move the pair. The stick, made from Douglas fir beams reinforced with steel, is 205 feet long. Cowichan Community Centre is at 2687 James Street.

- **The big hockey stick** at Hockey Plaza on Main Street in Eveleth, Minnesota. In June 2002, it replaced a smaller stick from 1995; the new one is 110 feet long, half the size of Duncan's. Behind the hockey stick are a large puck and a hockey mural.

Paul Bunyan and Babe the Blue Ox

Bemidji, Minnesota

Paul Bunyan is the perfect American roadside attraction. Because he is a mythical character, the giant statues are not constrained by regional boundaries or preconceptions of what he should look like, but they are inevitably tall, like a tall tale should be. An axe, red shirt, and beard are common but in no way mandatory. Mostly seen in the upper Midwest, where fellow lumberjacks are likely to live, Pauls can nonetheless be found from Maine to California.

Paul and Babe, welcoming visitors to Bemidji, Minnesota, since 1937, were among the first giant statues built to celebrate a region's heritage. *Bemidji Visitors & Convention Bureau*

Bemidji has long been a retreat for those who like to hunt, fish, or relax by a lake. Looking to attract more visitors in the fall of 1937, business owners planned a winter carnival. With lumber so integral to the region, the legendary woodsman Paul Bunyan was chosen as the mascot. A statue was built with the mayor as a model, except three times larger. Babe was modeled after the largest ox at the nearby Headwaters logging camp; its frame was covered with wool for padding and then canvas to look more real. Babe was mounted on a one-and-a-half-ton International truck for double duty in parades, but after years on the road, the ox was set next to Paul and given a new skin of concrete.

Bemidji's Paul and Babe statues were among the first giant statues built to celebrate a region's heritage. They were so popular that even *Life* magazine did a story. Today the pair stand next to the town's tourist information center and overlook Lake Bemidji. Next door is the Paul Bunyan Amusement Park, just one of the many attractions named for the famous lumberjack and his pet.

Minnesota has a number of Pauls plus renderings of his sweetheart, flashlight, baby shoe, and anchor. One place roadtrippers might not think to look is at the center of the world's largest shopping center—the Mall of America outside Minneapolis. Paul Bunyan's Log Chute ride features thirteen animated characters along a dark watercourse, including a sawmill worker, a skunk, an 18-foot-tall Paul, and a 12-foot-tall Babe. Each has a steel frame covered with fiberglass. Paul's mouth and head move; Babe snorts while moving forward as if pulling a stump.

STATS	Paul	Babe
SIZE:	18 feet tall	10 feet tall, 23 feet long
MADE OF:	wood frame, reinforcing bars, steel lath, stucco	wood, wire lath, concrete
BUILT:	1937	1937

If you visit . . .

Bemidji is at the intersection of U.S. Routes 2 and 71 in north-central Minnesota. Paul and Babe are at Third Street and Bemidji Avenue North, a.k.a. Paul Bunyan Drive, MN Route 197, and old U.S. Route 2. Across the street at Morell's Chippewa Trading Post, and next to a Maid-Rite loose-meat sandwich restaurant, is an Indian Muffler Man. Contact the Bemidji Tourist Information Center or the Bemidji Visitors and Convention Bureau.

www.visitbemidji.com

If you like Paul and Babe, you'll also like . . .

● The **animated Paul and Babe** in Paul Bunyan's Log Chute water ride are in Camp Snoopy, Mall of America, Bloomington, Minnesota, at the intersection of I-494 and MN Route 77, about fifteen minutes from both downtown Minneapolis and downtown St. Paul.
info.campsnoopy.com/Rides/Log Chute.htm

● The giant **Paul and Babe** among giant redwoods at Trees of Mystery, 15500 North Redwood Highway (U.S. Route 101), Klamath, California, a .8-mile walk-through attraction featuring trees in bizarre shapes ("awe-inspiring interpretives," the site calls them). The original Paul from 1947 was papier-mâché. A 35-foot-tall blue ox was added in 1949, and the current 49-foot, 2-inch Paul was raised in 1962. (They say he expands 3/4 inch taller on a hot day.) A great gift shop offers all sorts of redwood-themed souvenirs.
www.treesofmystery.com

● **The talking, blinking, arm-, head-, and mouth-moving Paul Bunyan** at Paul Bunyan Land, an amusement park at This Old Farm Pioneer Village, 17469 U.S. Route 18, seven miles east of Brainerd, Minnesota. The 36-foot-tall fiberglass Paul was moved from the nearby Paul Bunyan Amusement Center when it closed in 2003, after fifty-three years. He originally came from the Chicago & Northern Railway Company after being displayed at a railroad expo in Chicago in 1949. You'll also find Paul's pocketwatch, which once stood in town, and a coin-operated Babe ride.
www.thisoldfarm.net

Paul and Babe can also be found inside a water ride at the Mall of America in Bloomington, Minnesota. *Camp Snoopy, Mall of America*

After making their way thousands of miles west, Paul and Babe stand outside the Trees of Mystery in Klamath, California. *Photo by Sara Amy Leach*

- The **Babe** and **Muffler Man Paul** at Paul Bunyan Bowl, MN Routes 371 and 210 just west of Brainerd, Minnesota. It's near the former Paul Bunyan Amusement Center (now the site of Kohl's) and owned by the same family.

- The **kneeling Paul Bunyan** in Akeley, Minnesota, with outstretched palm, in front of the Paul Bunyan Historical Museum on Main Street, documenting the area's lumber history. The town's Paul Bunyan Days, held every June, were started in 1955 to help attract tourists.

- The **Paul and Babe** at Carson Park, 1110 Carson Park Drive, in Eau Claire, Wisconsin, built in 1982 for the Paul Bunyan Logging Camp, a themed area that teaches about the logging industry. A Tall Tales Room has an enormous replica of Paul's boot.
  www.paulbunyancamp.org

- The **fenced-in Babe and seated Paul** in the shadow of Castle Rock, an outcropping 3 miles north of St. Ignace, Michigan. Both have a bit of a stunned look on their concrete faces. A gift shop charges visitors 50¢ to go in back past the pair and climb the big rock, which overlooks Mackinac Island. On Business Loop I-75 or Exit 348 of I-75.

- **Paul and Babe** standing along U.S. Route 23 in Ossineke, Michigan, three miles south of the dinos and cave folk at Dinosaur Park.

- The 31-foot-tall **happy Paul** next to the Chamber of Commerce at 519 Main Street in Bangor, Maine, celebrates his "birthplace." He wears a big smile—perhaps because he recalls coming to life in Stephen King's novel, *IT*.
  www.bangorregion.com

Yes, Indiana, There Is a Santa Claus

Santa Claus, Indiana

DEDICATED
TO THE CHILDREN OF THE WORLD
IN
MEMORY OF AN UNDYING LOVE

DEC 25 1935

ou know a town with a name like Santa Claus is going to have fun with its unusual name. In the little village by that name in southern Indiana, there's Lake Rudolph Campground and RV Resort. There's a great old theme park, originally Santa Claus Land, that still has a Christmas area. There's Santa's Lodge on Christmas Boulevard, with not one but *two* Santa statues waiting to be added to your scrapbook album.

STATS

SIZE: 22 feet tall

MADE OF: concrete

BUILT: 1935

The oldest Santa in town is a statue overlooking the road east. Each side of its pedestal has an inscription, the front one proclaiming that it was dedicated to the children of the world on December 25, 1935. Another says, "There is nothing so universal as the spirit of Santa Claus." The base is in the shape of the Star of Bethlehem, with its main point showing the way east to the Holy Land.

Every year since 1983, the town's post office, on Kringle Place, has offered a picture postmark designed by an art contest winner from a local high school. Grown-ups send their letters here for the special postmark; kids send them to Santa, expecting an answer. The nonprofit Santas Elves are joined by the Christmas Lake Village Garden Club, the American Legion, Holiday World, and local senior citizens—just about everyone in the area—to send (and pay for) up to ten thousand replies each year, a tradition started by the postmaster in 1914. (To have your mail stamped with the special postmark between December 1 and 24, send it with postage already affixed, in a sturdy envelope or box to Postmaster, Santa Claus Station, Santa Claus, IN 47579-9998.)

The town also hosts a two-day festival every December. Surrounding towns such as Rockport hold celebrations too, as do attractions like the nearby Lincoln Boyhood National Memorial.

One of the early boosters was Louis Koch, who started Santa Claus Land as a retirement project. It opened on August 3, 1946, and the park's Freedom Train has operated since that day. Koch's son Bill and daughter-in-law Pat have been in the business for decades, and their son Will, who started his career by playing an elf, is now president and general manager. In 1984, Santa Claus Land added two new areas—Fourth of July and Halloween—and changed its name to Holiday World. Holidog's Funtown, added in 1999, includes its own giant: Holidog's Treehouse, the country's biggest family-play superstructure.

If you visit . . .

The town's Santa sits back from the road near the entrance to RoMar Construction Equipment Company on 69 South State Road 245. The town and attractions are six miles south of I-64, Exit 63. For more information, contact Spencer County Visitors Bureau.

Set back from the road, this statue still greets visitors to Santa Claus, Indiana.

www.legendaryplaces.org

Holiday World is on IN Route 162.

www.holidayworld.com

Just a few miles away on IN Route 162 is Lincoln State Park and the adjacent Lincoln Boyhood National Memorial, which preserves the farm where Abraham Lincoln lived from age seven to twenty-one (1816 to 1830), when his family moved to Illinois. It is also the gravesite of his mother.
www.nps.gov/libo

If you like Santa, you'll also like . . .

• The **Santas** of all sorts found at Santa's Workshop/North Pole amusement park in Manitou Springs, Colorado. This Christmas-themed park opened in 1956 at the foot of Pikes Peak (elevation 7,500 feet, barely halfway to the summit of 14,110). Holiday-themed rides and gift shops are spread across a shady mountainside. At the center is an ever-frozen North Pole, an actual pillar of ice; there's always a handprint or two melted into it (look for the kids walking around with cold hands). You can even meet Santa and some of his llamas (real

reindeer don't live in Colorado). The park is ten miles northwest of Colorado Springs, just west of Manitou Springs (filled with 1950s motels) off U.S. Route 24. From Denver, take I-25 south to Exit 141.
www.santas-colo.com

• **The World's Largest Santa Claus**, 48 feet tall and 33 feet wide, next to the Santa Claus House gift shop in North Pole, Alaska. He was built for the 1962 Seattle World's Fair. To restore Santa in December 2000, Hampton Hotels' Save-A-Landmark Program had to build a 60-foot-high tent around him, then heat it so he could be painted while outside temperatures hovered below zero. The gift shop grew from a small trading business that Con and Nellie Miller had started in the early 1950s among the villages of Alaska's interior. Con wore an old Santa suit, and when they began building a trading post in the new town of North Pole in 1952,

He sees you when you're sliding; a candy-cane-inspired slide at North Pole amusement park, Manitou Springs, Colorado.

kids would ask "Santa" if he was building a new house. Still in the family, the business has expanded to offer a full line of Alaskan gifts, Christmas ornaments, and toys. As in the town of Santa Claus, Indiana, many of the businesses here trade on the Christmas theme. The town is 13 miles east of Fairbanks on the Richardson Highway, which most tourists continue on after driving north on the Alaska, or Alcan, Highway. Santa Claus House is at 101 St. Nicholas Drive.
www.santaclaushouse.com

- The **Santa** at Magic Forest in Lake George, New York. Santa waves from just behind the giant Uncle Sam in the parking lot. The park opened in the 1960s as Christmas City/Santa's Village.

- The 18-foot-tall **rotund Santa** at the Rice Road exit of U.S. Route 101 in Oxnard, California. This Santa is better known from his home of fifty-two years in the chimney atop Santa's Candy Kitchen in Carpinteria, California. The roadside juice stand northwest of Los Angeles (about ten miles south of Santa Barbara) was started in 1948 by Ohio transplants June and Patrick McKeon. With Santa watching over it, their business grew from fruit, dates, nuts, and olives into a Christmas-themed attraction. The road out front, which became Santa Claus Lane, is still parallel to El Camino Real (U.S. Route 101), but pressure for upscale housing and commerce squeezed out the business and Santa. The late architectural historian David Gebhard was a leading advocate of granting it landmark status, but business pressures were too strong; those who thought the giant was a local icon were outnumbered (or at least outvoiced) by those who thought the statue too tacky for the seaside-themed community that had blossomed around it. Santa was taken down and plopped out back in March 2002, but he survived, and in January 2003, he was moved about 20 miles southwest to Oxnard. His plaster on wire mesh was patched, his paint freshened, and Santa now stands, fenced in, at a roadside rest area. Some three hundred people attended his dedication.

- **The 50-foot-tall snowman** on the southeast corner of Margaret Street and MN Route 36, the pride of North St. Paul, Minnesota.

- **The World's Largest Penguin**, which welcomes visitors to Cut Bank, Montana. This 27-foot-tall stucco-over-metal-frame bird, built by Ron Gustafson after the bitter winter of 1989, stands in front of his Glacier Gateway Inn and French Quarters restaurant at 1121 East Railroad Street. The town is west of I-15 along U.S. Route 2, about 22 miles south of the Canadian border and 45 miles east of Glacier National Park.
www.glaciergatewayinn.com

Brooks Catsup Bottle
Collinsville, Illinois

Fans young and old stop to snap pictures of the Collinsville catsup bottle.

he Brooks Catsup Bottle is so big, it could hold a hundred thousand gallons of ketchup. But it doesn't, as far as we know. . . .

The big bottle was built in 1949 to disguise a water tower at a Brooks Catsup factory. When a new company bought the plant in 1993, the bottle was nearly destroyed; it was no longer needed and was peeling and rusty.

Lots of folks in Collinsville had worked at the plant and began fund-raising to save the bottle—even the Brooks company and the new owners donated money. (Brooks catsup is still sold. The brand is now owned by Birds Eye Foods and made in Canada.) People volunteered a lot of time and raised more than $70,000 to repair, repaint, and maintain the water tower. In 1995, a parade and lighting ceremony celebrated its restoration. In 2002, it was named to the National Register of Historic Places. And every year, the town holds a big birthday bash for the bottle with a car show, hula hoop contest, and water balloon games.

Water towers, usually the tallest structures around, are often used to celebrate a local product. You can visit water towers masquerading as an ear of corn (Rochester, Minnesota), an apple and a pumpkin (Jackson and Circleville, Ohio), a peach (Clanton, Alabama, and Gaffney, South Carolina), a strawberry (Poteet, Texas), and an egg (Newberry, South Carolina).

STATS

SIZE: 170 feet high (a 70-foot bottle atop a 100-foot pole), bottle diameter 25 feet, cap diameter 8 feet

MADE OF: riveted steel

BUILT: 1949

If you visit . . .

The bottle towers over the plant at 800 South Morrison Avenue (IL Route 159), just south of downtown Collinsville. Souvenirs can be found at Ashmann's Pharmacy, 209 East Main Street. Both the National Road and Historic Route 66 run through town, which sits about a dozen miles east of St. Louis (about 5 miles south of I-70/I-55 and 5 miles north of I-64). Check the website of the World's Largest Catsup Bottle International Fan Club.

www.catsupbottle.com

If you like the Catsup Bottle, you'll also like . . .

- The pair of 35-foot-long **Heinz Ketchup bottles** atop the scoreboard at Heinz Field on North Shore Drive in Pittsburgh. When the Steelers move the football into their opponents' "red zone"—the 20 yard line to the goal—the bottles tilt over and fill the scoreboard's "Heinz Red Zone" with virtual ketchup.

- The 3-foot-tall **tomato** sitting west of Indianapolis on Rockville Road.

- The **Vess soda bottle** at Sixth and O'Fallon Streets in St. Louis. The 1952 bottle, 25 1/2 feet tall on a 12-foot pole, was moved in 1967. It was renovated in about 1990, its neon outline restored. It can be seen from I-70 west.

- The three massive **Coke bottles** outside the Coca-Cola bottling plant at 1334 South Central Avenue, south of the Produce District in Los Angeles, added when the building was expanded in 1941. The 1936–37 building is shaped like a streamlined ocean liner. It's nicknamed the SS *Coca Cola*.

Dueling Donuts

Los Angeles, California

onuts are big in Los Angeles. They're popular, too. According to a 1997 survey by *Bakery Production and Marketing Magazine*, one-sixth of all donut shops in the United States are located in the five-county Los Angeles area. That's more per capita than anywhere else in the country, earning it the title of America's Donut Capital. Perhaps it's because the short list of ingredients—flour, sugar, shortening, leavening, egg, milk, and flavoring—and the simplicity of creating the deep-fried treats makes donuts a popular start-up business for immigrants.

The Big Do-Nut Drive-In chain is no longer with us, but its rooftop donuts live on in larger-than-life snackdom. The first was built in 1950 and survives the chain's demise

STATS	Big Do-Nuts	Donut Hole
SIZE (diameter):	32¹/₂ feet	40 feet
MADE OF:	concrete	fiberglass
BUILT:	early 1950s	1968

as Kindle's Do-nuts. Getting more publicity is one renamed Randy's Donuts; it's near Los Angeles International Airport, making for a popular photo op of an airplane spied through the donut's hole. Owners Larry and Ron Weintraub maintain its high profile with appearances in everything from music videos to movies such as *Coming to America*. A commercial on their website shows the ring-shaped giant crashing down and rolling away. The diameter that most sources give, 22 feet, always seemed short relative to the people standing below, so we asked Larry. He and his brother climbed up on the roof for us with a tape measure and, sure enough, they found it to be 32½ feet across. Another of the chain survives as Donut King II, and one more is rumored to remain in Compton; seven others have disappeared. Competitors also arose, such as the Do-Nut Hole in the City of Industry.

The Donut Hole in La Puente gives new meaning to the term drive-through. Photo by Rick Sebak

Those big donuts could be topped only by ones so gargantuan that a car could drive through them; such was the size of the Donut Hole drive-throughs. The first opened in Covina in 1963, and the owners were soon granted U.S. patent number D199,303. In 1968, they opened another in La Puente, getting patent number D215,540. When the chain dissolved in 1979, the La Puente drive-through was sold, the Covina one remodeled, and three others demolished. At La Puente, you drive through the hole of a giant chocolate donut to enter a tunnel lined with display windows, get your order, and drive out through another donut. The pastry's innards are used for storage. Like Randy's, the Donut Hole is a popular place for photos; newlyweds in particular like to drive their wedding parties through the attraction.

If you visit . . .

Kindle's Do-nuts is at 10003 South Normandie Avenue at West Century Boulevard, Los Angeles.

Randy's is at 805 West Manchester Boulevard at La Cienega Boulevard, Inglewood. It sells mugs, hats, and

Randy's, perhaps the most famous donut shop, in Inglewood, California. *Photo by Rick Sebak*

Maple Donuts on U.S. Route 30 in York, Pennsylvania, has another big donut holding its mailbox.

T-shirts, or you can check out their donut offerings online.

www.randysdonuts.com

The rooftop Big Do-Nut giant at 15032 South Western Avenue in Gardena has been repainted yellow with "Donut King II" in red.

The Donut Hole at 15300 East Amar Road near North Hacienda Boulevard and East Elliot Avenue in La Puente, is open round the clock.

If you like these Donuts, you'll also like . . .

- The **big donuts** of the small chain of Maple Donuts in York, Pennsylvania. Some of the shops feature big donuts (though not as massive as the California variety) either on the roof or as roadside enticement.

- The **big donuts** atop the signs of DeAngelis Donuts in Rochester, northwest of Pittsburgh.

- The big, **flat-sided donut** that was part of a 1965 sign towering above Winchell's Donut House on Foothill Boulevard (old U.S. Route 66) in Upland, California. The donut is now looking for a new home. Two years of negotiations after the lease expired could not be resolved, and the store was demolished in March 2004. (Interestingly, city planners *encourage* nostalgic signs and architecture on this famous street.) Winchell's donated the sign, featuring neon letters and a Googie triangle, to the Route 66 Mother Road Museum in the restored 1911 Casa del Desierto (one of the famed Harvey House railside restaurants) in nearby Barstow. The museum does not have enough room, though, and has stored the donut at a car dealership until a new home is found. Winchell's, founded in 1948, is the West Coast's largest donut chain and has locations in Guam, New Zealand, Saipan, and Saudi Arabia.

Albert the Bull

Audubon, Iowa

Albert the Bull, a 30-foot-tall Hereford in Audubon, Iowa, honors the area's cattlemen.

lbert stands in such splendid shape today that it's hard to believe he's more than forty years old. His story goes back even farther. Cattle have long been shipped from this area to Chicago by rail—about fifty carloads each year. In 1951, local shippers invited Audubon banker Albert Kruse to accompany them as they rode in the caboose. He declined, knowing how unpleasant the trip could be on a cold fall day, but told them he'd go if they had a Pullman car. That's just what they got him, and the annual comfortable trip for shippers and businessmen became known as Operation T-Bone. It was a hit then and is still celebrated every September.

The idea for a giant statue to salute the cattle industry came ten years later, from Donald Oleson, but didn't take off until a Junior Chamber of Commerce

(Jaycees) was formed in 1963. Locals thought it dovetailed nicely with Operation T-Bone, believing it would make a good tourist attraction, and they decided to honor T-Bone originator Albert Kruse by naming the big bull for him.

The $30,000 needed to build Albert was obtained through fund-raisers and agricultural industry donations from across the nation. Once a concrete pad was poured, a frame of I-beams was built. The Jaycees rounded up steel rods from abandoned windmills and welded them together off-site, then placed the sections on the frame. The bull's head, one of four sections, was lifted on last. The outline was covered with wire mesh, then concrete was troweled over it. Two more layers of concrete were sprayed on to give it a hairlike texture. Sixty-five gallons of dark red and white paint completed the obviously male, 45-ton Hereford. Albert was dedicated on October 31, 1964, to coincide with the town's fourteenth annual Operation T-Bone. A kiosk has photos and a brief history.

The idea that the "world's largest bull" might bring tourists worked: More than twenty thousand people visit Albert every year.

If you visit . . .

The giant bull can be found in Albert the Bull Park, along U.S. Route 71 just south of downtown Audubon in west-central Iowa. The location of Albert was a question on the TV game show "Jeopardy!"

An approaching storm doesn't bother the mascot of the Cedar Crest Ice Cream plant at 2000 South Tenth St., Manitowoc, Wisconsin. *Photo by Shannon Jackson Arnold*

Gerald Bomba stares down a cow at an auction house on U.S. Route 19, Mercer, Pennsylvania.
Photo by Carol Bomba

If you like Albert, you'll also like . . .

- The big cows found all over Wisconsin. There's a **giant cow** at the Cedar Crest ice cream plant in Manitowoc, **Sissy** at Ehlenbach's Cheese Chalet in DeForest, and 30-foot-tall **Chatty Belle**, the "world's largest talking cow," in Neillsville. Chatty chats up locally made cheese. She's next to a replica of the onetime world's largest piece of cheese; the original was eaten in 1966, but its stunt double lounges in an air-conditioned Cheesemobile.

- The 12-foot-tall **white-faced Hereford** steer standing on a small trailer in front of the Big Texan Steak Ranch, "Home of the Free 72 oz. Steak." Challengers have one hour to eat the entire meal; about one out of six do, though the success rate for women is 50 percent. Losers pay the $50 tab. As for the big guy, sales manager Kathie Greer told us: "Anatomically, it's agreed that this is a boy bovine. On closer inspection, we know that he's been separated from the parts that make him virile and attractive to the girl cows (or heifers); however, we still refer to him around here as 'the Bull' so that his feelings don't get hurt." One of the owners, whose father founded the steakhouse, says that back when the steer arrived, he was called Big Moo. The mobile mascot makes appearances, too, and Kathy describes it better than we can: "These days you can see our bovine sign scootin' down the streets of area towns in parades touting rodeos, ding-dong daddies, and shamrocks." The restaurant and adjoining motel with Old West façade are at 7701 East I-40 in Amarillo, Texas.
  www.bigtexan.com

you can spot a Pal's restaurant by its rooftop food. The giant snacks distinguish the company from other chains, but the difference goes deeper.

Fred "Pal" Barger had seen a quick-service carryout in 1952 while stationed in Austin, Texas. Inspired, he launched his own place in Kingsport in 1956, and two years later, he took over the Arctic ice cream stand on Lynn Garden Drive. These two locations served him well for a quarter century, but Pal began searching for a way to transform them into drive-through locations. Thom Crosby joined the company with the goal of having Pal's surpass bigger chains in both food quality and efficiency.

One day Pal had dinner with artists Karen and Tony Barone, contemporaries of pop artists like Andy Warhol and Roy Lichtenstein. Tony used a napkin to sketch a stair-stepped building topped by gargantuan, colorful food. The restaurants would break the boundaries of design and signage—or at least bend them the way Programatic buildings had done before. This was not being done so much by the 1980s. In fact, Pal's Sudden Service outlets debuted in an era when such displays had become the bane of planning commissions and town beautification programs. Rooftop food may not be considered tasteful by some officials, but Pal forged ahead. His reason? "People love to be entertained."

Pal's Sudden Service restaurants feature not only giant food on the roof, but also food-shaped signs for drive-through customers. *Pal's*

The first Pal's drive-throughs opened in 1985 at Colonial Heights and Stone Drive. The company has since grown to seventeen locations centered around Kingsport. Customer—and employee—satisfaction consistently rates far above average for the industry. Pal's accomplishes this by the exhaustive collection and interpretation of data. Most amazing is that every owner-operator must devote part of every workday to "marketing by wandering around"—that is, talking to employees and customers. They also must go door-to-door within a 3-mile radius of their restaurants to learn what potential customers want and current customers think.

All this dedication to principles culminated in the company's receiving the Malcolm Baldrige National Quality Award in 2001, the first, and still the only, restaurant company to win. The program raises awareness that excellence in quality and performance gives companies a competitive edge. The award is managed by the U.S. Commerce Department's National Institute of Standards and Technology; it was presented to Pal's by President George W. Bush.

One Pal's location has a Muffler Man. "Big Pal" was added in 1962 to the company's second store rooftop at 1316 Lynn Garden Drive, just south of Weber City, Virginia. The location was remodeled in 2002 but Big Pal remains, dressed in all white and holding a big burger. As for the rooftop food, Thom Crosby, now president and CEO, told us they are washed monthly and waxed yearly.

If you visit . . .

Pal's are located throughout eastern Tennessee and southwestern Virginia. The company is headquartered at 327 Revere Street, Kingsport, in the northeastern corner of Tennessee.

www.palsweb.com

STATS	Hot Dog	Hamburger	Frenchie Fries	Cup of Tea
SIZE:	21 feet wide, 3 feet high	20 feet wide, 4 feet high	6.5 feet high	8 feet high
MADE OF:	fiberglass	fiberglass	aluminum	aluminum
BUILT:	1985–present			

A big bag draws shoppers to the Market Place grocery store in Jackson, Tennessee. *Photo by Claudette Stager*

A big burger makes it hard to miss Max & Erma's restaurant in downtown Pittsburgh.

If you like Pal's, you'll also like . . .

- **Big food** in the sky at the Market Place grocery at 1727 South Highland Avenue in Jackson, Tennessee.

- **The big burger**, which measures 6 feet, 4 inches high and 8 feet wide, at Max & Erma's, 630 Stanwix Street in Pittsburgh. The burger debuted in 1998. A similar one was installed the following year outside corporate offices, 4849 Evanswood Drive, Columbus, Ohio.

- **The antique stove** towering over the Michigan State Fairgrounds in Detroit, at 25 feet high, 20 feet wide, 30 feet long, and 15 tons. The wooden icon was painted to look like metal for a company's exhibit at the 1893 World's Columbian Exposition in Chicago. Afterward, it went to the company in Detroit, and in 1965, it moved to the fairgrounds; deterioration forced its disassembly in 1974. Starting in 1988, fair management and local supporters raised funds and restored the icon, unveiling it on August 24, 1998.

- Three **cup-shaped restaurants** from the 1940s in eastern Pennsylvania, remnants of Levengood Dairy Farms of Pottstown. The round steel-covered buildings have straws pointing out the tops, but they've been remodeled. One in Boyertown has served various owners and may be closed. The cup at 427 Pottstown Avenue in Pennsburg is now a Rita's Italian Ices. The Pottstown Cup, 903 Charlotte Street, has been rehabbed with a nostalgic theme that draws customers to its breakfasts and diner-type food. **www.pottstowncup.com**

Lucy the Elephant

Margate, New Jersey

For more than a century, Lucy, the grande dame of roadside giants, has watched over the shore at Margate, New Jersey. *Photo by Kyle Weaver*

t was about 1880. Twenty-four-year-old real estate speculator James Lafferty wanted to sell land for summer homes along the shores of South Atlantic City, but he needed to attract buyers. His solution—a gargantuan elephant—may not be the first idea most people would have, but it worked. It lured vacationers down to the swampy area by rail and steamer, and once folks were inside its belly or up in its howdah, Lafferty could show them the land. Though it cost $38,000 (about $700,000 today), the elephant proved to be a wise investment.

Lucy worked so well that Lafferty designed two more, both started in 1884. The larger of them was built on Surf Avenue in Coney Island, across from Manhattan. At 122 feet tall, it was twice the size of Lucy–so big that it had thirty-one rooms. One leg even contained a cigar store. Lafferty sold the building rights for the smaller of the two, to be built at South Cape May, a seaside resort farther down the Jersey shore. Both were financial failures and survived only a short time. The Coney Island colossus burnt down in 1896, and the Cape May one was torn down in 1900.

After serving only a few years as a real estate office, Lucy was sold to the Gertzen family. She was opened as a tourist attraction at 10¢ a tour. By 1902, she'd been converted to a summer cottage. A storm the following year left her mired in sand; workers somehow dug her out and moved her inland about fifty feet. In 1909, the name of South Atlantic City was changed to Margate, after a famous resort in England.

Following a particularly bad storm in 1962, Lucy was left with gaping holes. In 1970, descendants of the Gertzen family donated Lucy to the city of Margate but sold the land to developers, placing her at risk if she could not be relocated. The Margate Civic Association had been formed in the months leading up to this, partly so funds could be raised before Lucy was razed. City-owned beach-front property was secured two blocks to the southwest. The challenge of moving the rickety wooden building spurred the formation of the Save Lucy Committee, which was then given just thirty days to raise the thousands of dollars needed to move her.

Thanks to the Herculean efforts of friends and fans, everything was ready for the proposed moving day of July 20, 1970, but three days before the move, a landowner filed suit that its holdings would lose value if Lucy was moved near them. A hearing was scheduled, but it would not take place until one day *after* the thirty-day deadline. A special Saturday hearing had to be arranged, and Save Lucy supporters won. Everyone got back to work, and on Monday, July 20, the move was made. Lucy, up on dollies, was pulled down the street by a pickup truck. The group got Lucy listed in the National Register of Historic Places in 1971, but hundreds of thousands of dollars were still needed to restore the structure, including replacing its metal skin and howdah. In 1976, she received a prestigious National Historic Landmark designation.

Thousands of visitors every year tour Lucy. A staircase in each hind leg (one to enter, one to exit) leads to the main room in her belly. There you can see old photos, souvenirs, and a video about the elephant's history. Smaller rooms surround the main one, and the head has a lookout platform. More staircases lead to the howdah on her back, where visitors can again look out across the ocean and the town that grew from the swamps. We're told there are 350 steps from the ground to the howdah. Improvements are planned to make the site handicapped-accessible while maintaining a close-to-original appearance. At six stories tall, Lucy still attracts a lot of attention, making her perhaps the best known of the roadside giants.

If you visit . . .

Lucy is about 2 miles south of Atlantic City, along the beach at 9200 Atlantic Avenue between Washington and Decator Avenues in Margate—you'll see her. A website for the giant pachyderm has a detailed history, the source for much of our information, and offers Lucy-themed coffee mugs, ceramic miniatures, sun catchers, rubber erasers, and temporary tattoos.
    www.lucytheelephant.org

If you like Lucy the Elephant, you'll also like . . .

● The 10-foot-tall **pink elephant** east of Huntington, West Virginia, on the north side of U.S. Route 60. It reportedly was built about 1980 by a local couple in celebration of their granddaughter's birth. It's near Barboursville, a few miles east of I-64.

A pink elephant—large, though perhaps not by elephant standards—stands east of Huntington, West Virginia, along U.S. Route 60.

- **Pinky**, a larger, more realistic pink elephant standing outside the Isle of Capri Casino in Marquette, Iowa, along the banks of the Upper Mississippi River. Pinky started out decades ago as a gray-colored mascot for a Republican convention in Sparta, Wisconsin. It was repainted when it moved to the Pink Elephant Supper Club. Pinky's biggest adventure was riding a pontoon boat downriver in 1976 to see presidential candidate Jimmy Carter. When Isle of Capri Casino opened in September 2000, Pinky became its mascot, albeit with a Caribbean makeover. The street address is 100 Anti Monopoly.

- **The Partying Pink Elephant** at the Interstate (Phillips) 66 service complex, 4995 County Road V off I-90/94, Exit 126 north, DeForest, Wisconsin, near Madison. This elephant wears sunglasses, apparently for the morning after.

- The glasses-wearing **pink elephant drinking from a wine glass** outside Wagon Wheel Liquors at 308 West Broadway Street, Fortville, Indiana.

- **Miss Ellie Phunt** at Mr. Ed's Elephant Museum, between the original and rerouted Lincoln Highway west of Gettysburg, at 6016 Chambersburg Road (U.S. Route 30), Orrtanna, Pennsylvania. Six thousand other elephant souvenirs are on display and there's a huge selection of candy and nuts for sale.

- The 67½-foot-tall **giraffe** outside the Dallas Zoo at 650 South R. L. Thornton Freeway (I-35E), the tallest statue in Texas. Its metal skeleton was covered with urethane foam and fiberglass, coated with a gel of 80 percent bronze, then buffed to create an antique finish. For a brief while in 1994, a new 67-foot Sam Houston statue in Huntsville was taller, so the giraffe was given a tongue extension, bringing the statue to its current height and recapturing the state record.
  www.dallas-zoo.org

- **Nipper, dog mascot of RCA** and "his master's voice," cocking his head above 991 Broadway north of downtown Albany, New York. He was erected in 1954 atop the former RTA Building, the local RCA distributor, and once had the accompanying Victrola and horn. When Arnoff Moving & Storage took over the building in the late 1990s, it spruced up the 25-foot-high, four ton dog statue, which is fiberglass over steel mesh and an iron frame. Roadside fans who want a snack after seeing Nipper can visit the Miss Albany Diner, 893 Broadway.

The Blue Whale
Catoosa, Oklahoma

This happy whale along the original path of U.S. Route 66 in Catoosa, Oklahoma, has recently been restored. *Photo by Guy Randall*

oadside fans, especially those of the fabled Route 66, have had a number of heartbreaks in recent years. The Club Café and its "fatman" signs in Santa Rose, New Mexico. Pop hicks Restaurant in Clinton, Oklahoma. Coral Court in St. Louis. And for a long time, the Blue Whale was going the way of so many other great old attractions, closed and fading back into the land. But locals could not let that happen; in 1997, volunteers and the Catoosa Chamber of Commerce started cleaning up, and today it's a roadside success story.

Zelta Davis collected whale figures. In 1970, her husband, Hugh, began building the big whale on their pond as an anniversary gift. He had been a zookeeper, and they already had a reptile farm and ark on their property, used mostly for kids' parties. (Across the road was a trading post run by Chief Wolf-Robe Hunt,

STATS

SIZE: 80 feet long

MADE OF: wood, rebar, wire mesh, concrete

BUILT: 1970–72

Zelta's brother.) Visitors enjoyed swimming in the pond, and the whale drew new crowds to slide from its side or dive off its high tail. Portholes in the whale's second story could be reached from a ladder.

The beach closed in 1988, and after Davis died, the whale deteriorated. The water became dirty, and signs warned that trespassers would be shot. The first renovation efforts in 1997 helped, and then in 2002, new paint, plumbing, and landscaping brought the site back to life. The whale was featured in a Zippy the Pinhead comic strip that July 15, and Hampton Inn's Save-A-Landmark volunteers helped too. The Blue Whale wears a baseball cap again, and a new Route 66 roadside attraction sign welcomes tourists.

The Davises' children now operate the attraction, but on a smaller scale. Swimming is no longer allowed, but guests can visit the smiling whale for free and eat snacks on one of its stools supported by little concrete whales. The restrooms have also been restored. You can even buy a cool Catoosa whale T-shirt. The trading post building across the road remains, but as an auto parts shop.

Brush has been cleared around the ark, but it continues to decay, much as the whale once did. The Blue Whale, however, again welcomes happy picnickers and fans of roadside attractions.

If you visit . . .

The whale is along Old U.S. Highway 66, just off OK Route 66 (historic U.S. Route 66), about a mile northeast of Catoosa, which is east of Tulsa, Oklahoma, and just north of I-44/U.S. Route 412 (Exit 241). A 1913 iron truss bridge with plank flooring crosses Spunky Creek half a mile south of the whale.

If you like the Blue Whale, you'll also like . . .

- The **life-size sperm whale** outside the Science Center of Connecticut at 950 Trout Brook Drive in West Hartford. The adult male, made in 1976 with 15 tons of cement, is 60 feet long, 15 feet tall, and 15 feet wide—large enough to fit twenty-nine people inside. His name is Conny, short for Connecticut, whose official state animal is the sperm whale. The whale was refurbished and rededicated in 1996 with help from the Cetacean Society International, which had helped build it twenty years earlier. The redo included a spout to shoot water.

- **Swampy the Alligator**, which holds the admission counter, gift shop, and offices of Jungle Adventures (originally Gatorland), a 20-acre wildlife sanctuary and alligator farm that has operated in Christmas, Florida, since the 1970s. Swampy, built in 1992, is 200 feet and 1 inch long. Jungle Adventures is 17 miles east of Orlando at 26205 East FL Route 50. www.jungleadventures.com

- **The Second Largest Alligator** at Jungleland (formerly Alligatorland Safari Zoo) and the Gator Motel, 4580 West U.S. Route 192 in Kissimmee, Florida. The 126-foot-long reptile was once the largest gator until Swampy was built.

At least a half-dozen marriage ceremonies have taken place in the mouth of the Shrine to Anglers at the National Fresh Water Fishing Hall of Fame in Hayward, Wisconsin. *Photo by Rick Sebak*

- The walk-in-mouth, 65-foot-long, 14-foot-tall **muskie** between Bemidji and Grand Rapids at 456 U.S. Route 2 NE, a few miles west of Bena, Minnesota. It was built in 1958 as the Big Fish Drive Inn. Its teeth are regularly stolen, so they were left in only during the summer months, when a handwritten note implored, "Please Do Not Damage Teeth." The fish was sold in 2002 and has been closed in recent years.

- The 26-foot-long **fiberglass walleye** in Garrison, Minnesota, built in 1965 to celebrate the town's self-proclaimed status as "Walleye Pike Capital of the World." The town indeed sits along the most popular walleye lake in the state, Mille Lacs.

- The 65-foot-long **leaping salmon** at the Atlanta Fish Market, 265 Pharr Road, east of Peachtree, Georgia. It was built in 1995 of solid copper.

- The **giant crab** on the roof of the Giant Crab Seafood Restaurant, at 9597 North Kings Highway (U.S. Route 17), Myrtle Beach, South Carolina. The crab overlooks the Intercoastal Waterway in the Restaurant Row section of town. www.giantcrab.com

- The realistic, 20-foot-long **giant lobster** at Ruth and Wimpy's Kitchen, 792 U.S. Route 1, Hancock, Maine. The lobster is nicknamed Wilbur after the owners' last name.

- The **giant blue claw crab and pink shrimp** overlooking Gaido's Seafood Restaurant (crab on roof) and Casey's Seafood Café (shrimp on a pole), operated by the Gaido family on the Galveston Seawall at 3800–3802 Seawall Boulevard in Galveston, Texas. The family restaurant business was started by great-grandfather S. J. Gaido in 1911. www.galveston.com/gaidos/restaurants.html and www.caseysseafoodcafe.com

Koontz Coffee Pot
Bedford, Pennsylvania

THE
COFFEE
POT

ike so many roadside buildings-as-things, the Coffee Pot on the west end of Bedford thrived in its early years, drawing traffic from the Lincoln Highway, the premier transcontinental road. Coffeepots were a popular café motif, whether as a sign, sprouting from the roof, or serving as the building itself. Bert Koontz built this one adjacent to his gas station in 1927, about the time the road was adopting its new federal designation, U.S. Route 30. The Pot thrived as a business and landmark along the highway until 1940, when the Pennsylvania Turnpike opened parallel to Route 30 in the central and western part of the state. Despite its tolls, drivers liked the turnpike's more direct route, gentler hills, and increased speeds. When a Route 30 bypass later opened around Bedford, the Coffee Pot and nearby road-dependent businesses suffered even more. After decades as a lively tavern, the Coffee Pot closed and fell into disrepair.

STATS

SIZE: 18 feet tall

MADE OF: wood framing covered by tar paper, later by stucco on metal lath

BUILT: 1927

In 2000, the Lashley family, owners of the Coffee Pot and adjacent station let the Lincoln Highway Heritage Corridor conduct a feasibility study for restoring the Pot. They eventually decided to move it across the road and about a quarter mile east to the county fairgrounds. It was lifted and trucked through a snowstorm in December 2003, and restoration was soon under way. Architect Michael Eversmeyer told us about several structural problems in a letter:

The Coffee Pot, spiffed up and at its new home in Bedford, Pennsylvania. *Lincoln Highway Heritage Corridor*

The first floor had collapsed into the crawl space, and the second floor later collapsed and had to be replaced. There were holes in the exterior stucco skin, especially where the building had been struck by cars and trucks; bees were nesting in the walls; most of the windows and their frames were rotted; about a third of the roof overhang had rotted away completely; and the bottom ends of most of the studs had suffered rot damage. Inside, a fifteen-footwide section of the exterior wall, two stories in height, had been removed to create a new opening between the Coffee Pot and a new hotel lobby/bar.

There had never been an exterior entrance to the Coffee Pot; since the Coffee Pot was now to be freestanding, I had to design a doorway. I located it where the original interior doorway had been, adapting the design of the window frames.

Originally, the Pot was covered by tar paper painted silver-gray to simulate the appearance of a metal coffeepot. In the 1940s, the tar paper was covered with a half-inch-thick layer of stucco on metal lath, which was scored and colored to resemble the brick that was used to face the adjacent building and the new hotel behind the Coffee Pot. This stucco likely saved the Coffee Pot for posterity, but it was in bad shape. I specified the installation of new metal lath over the entire building, including the remaining stucco, and application of a new layer of stucco to be finished smooth and painted silver-gray. We ended up with a close resemblance to the original building (including its slightly irregular surface) while using a durable historically appropriate material.

The roof framing was retained in its entirety, though the overhang had to be rebuilt. We reroofed with rolled roofing, replaced porcelain light sockets under the overhang, and installed a new wooden ball at the apex of the roof/lid. I estimate that we probably saved about half of the original structure, and replaced the rest to match the original.

With help from state and federal grants, the Lincoln Highway Heritage Corridor restored the Coffee Pot and dedicated it in August 2004. The final touch was added by local artist and roadside fan Kevin Kutz, who painted "The Coffee Pot" in lettering just like the original. In 2005, the Pot was listed in the National Register of Historic Places. The Bedford County Fairgrounds Association will host exhibits on the history of the fair inside and hopes to add a gift shop. Meanwhile, travelers continue to do what they have for eight decades: stop and snap pictures.

If you visit . . .

The Coffee Pot towers over the entrance of the Bedford County Fairgrounds, Business U.S. Route 30 on the west end of Bedford, Pennsylvania, just a few blocks from the dazzling Art Deco Dunkle's Gulf.
   www.lhhc.org

If you like the Coffee Pot, you'll also like . . .

• The 12-foot-tall **Chester Teapot**, in Chester, West Virginia, originally built as a root beer barrel in Oakdale, Pennsylvania. It was moved and converted in 1938 to sell snacks and advertise an adjacent pottery business, the area's leading industry. (Homer Laughlin China still makes Fiesta ware nearby.) The restored red and white teapot now sits at the U.S. Route 30 exit ramp, but an accompanying creamer has gone missing.

• The **two-story coffeepot-shaped building** used by the James River Basin Canoe Livery in central Virginia between Lexington and Buena Vista, 1870 East Midland Trail (U.S. Route 60), 1.5 miles east of I-81 Exit 188-A, and 7 miles west of the Blue Ridge Parkway. This coffeepot is covered in corrugated metal. www.canoevirginia.com

• **Bob's Java Jive**, 2102 South Tacoma Way in Tacoma, Washington. This building looks more like a 25-foot-tall teapot than a coffeepot, perhaps because its name comes from a 1950s Ink Spots song, not from the café's specialty. Like Koontz's, this pot was built in 1927. It's the last giant on the street, which once had a castle, a gas-pump-shaped service station, and the lemon-shaped Lemon Lunch.

• The 8-foot-tall **red coffeepot** pouring water into a yellow cup outside Lynn's Paradise Café, 984 Barret Avenue, Louisville, Kentucky.

• **The oldest oversize coffeepot**, sitting on a pole in Moravian Village of Old Salem, Winston-Salem, North Carolina. It was built about 1860 to advertise a silversmith.

Sapp Brothers use variations of a coffeepot to announce their travel centers throughout the Midwest; this one is at I-80 Exit 440 near Omaha.

On the other side of the country, Bob's Java Jive draws a crowd in Tacoma, Washington. *Photo by Doug Towne*

- The **Swedish coffeepot** in Kingsburg, California. In 1985, the town's chamber refashioned its 1911 water tower to celebrate local heritage. The 122-foot-tall tower got floral embellishments, as well as a handle and spout.

- The **Swedish coffeepot** in Stanton, Iowa. This water tower at the corner of Highland and Hilltop Avenues was rethemed partly because of the town's roots, but moreso because the town was the birthplace of the late actress Virginia Christine, whose role as Mrs. Olson in Folger's coffee commercials was her claim to fame, although she also appeared in 150 movies and 300 television shows. As marshal of the town's centennial parade in 1970, Christine served coffee to the public, and by the following year, the town had remade its tower in her honor. Atop a 90-foot-high tower is a 35-foot-tall pot holding 40,000 gallons of water. A matching water tower designed as a cup sitting on a saucer was added in 2000 and holds 150,000 gallons.

- **Bono's Historic Orange**, one of the few remaining orange-shaped orange juice stands, at Bono's Restaurant & Deli, 15395 Foothill Boulevard (Historic Route 66) in Ontario, California, built in 1936 and the huge fiberglass roof of **Orange World** in Kissimmee, Florida, shaped like the top half of an orange, at 5395 West Irlo Bronson Highway (US Route 192) a couple miles east of Disney World.
  www.orangeworld192.com

Airplane Station

Powell, Tennessee

Just north of Knoxville sits one of the last unrestored roadside giants. Others have been destroyed, and the few that survive usually have been rehabbed in some way. Most often they gain a spot in a city park or become the headquarters for a local historical group, though sometimes they're able to continue serving a commercial purpose. This Airplane Station has persevered, and it gives us all a chance to watch—and support—its restoration.

By the late 1920s, some states were signing the old named trails with the route numbers. The Clinton Highway north of Knoxville, now U.S. Route 25, had just been widened and christened TN Route 9. That's when Elmer and Henry Nickle decided to build their eye-catching station. Elmer's interest in aviation combined with the penchant of the day for building-as-sign led to the design of the "Aeroplane" Gasoline Service Building, as the blueprint called it. Miraculously, the plans—and even an invoice for the lumber—have

STATS

SIZE: 52 feet long, wings 12 feet wide, wingspan 42 feet

MADE OF: wood framing and beaded board paneling interior

BUILT: 1930

survived and are safely archived in the McClung Historical Collection at the Knox County Public Library in Knoxville. The station's office was in the cockpit, and the wings provided shelter for cars at the pumps. The brothers had business cards with the airplane on one side and their friend "Colonel" Harland Sanders on the other; his restaurant, north on U.S. Route 25 West in Corbin, Kentucky, would evolve into Kentucky Fried Chicken.

Henry and Elmer (dressed in flyer gear) Nickle on opening day, 1930, at their new station. *Calvin M. McClung Historical Collection, Knox County Public Library System*

After closing and being sold in the 1970s, the Airplane was home to a variety of businesses, most recently remodeled as the office for a used-car lot. To the rescue has come the Airplane Filling Station Preservation Association, whose members hope to save, restore, and reuse the building. The nonprofit group got it listed in the National Register of Historic Places and is also working with Knox Heritage, a state-sponsored local preservation group. They have held public meetings to discuss the Airplane's restoration and reuse. According to Dr. Tim Ezzell, Director of the Community Partnership Center at the University of Tennessee in Knoxville, who assisted the efforts: "Suggestions have included things like a pub or a coffeehouse, but I don't think the site's constraints will permit these. I personally think it may wind up as an office for a community or civic group."

The cost of evaluating and remediating possible soil contamination from underground tanks is an obstacle for anyone wanting to buy a vintage service station. Luckily, the issue of leaking underground storage tanks (LUST, for short—really) has already been addressed: The association was able to use a state program to test, fill, and cap the tanks, and the site has been cleaned.

The property owner is supportive and has signed a contract to sell the station to the group before the estimated $20,000 for restoration has even been raised. The group is currently seeking support through grants and donations.

The Airplane Service Station north of Knoxville, Tennessee, awaits restoration. *Photo by Tim Ezzell*

The Airplane Station, even now, looks a lot like N-X-211, *The Spirit of St. Louis*. In 1927, Charles Lindbergh and his plane were the first to fly nonstop from New York to Paris. They became the most recognizable duo in the world, inspiring millions of people, including perhaps a couple of service station owners.

If you visit . . .

The Airplane Station is at 6829 Clinton Highway, U.S. Route 25 West, Powell, Tennessee. "Help Save the Plane" T-shirts are $20 on the AFSPA website.
www.powellairplane.org

If you like the Airplane Station, you'll also like . . .

● **Art Lacey's Bomber Service Station**, long closed but mostly still there, with a B-17G bomber above its office, at 13515 Southeast McLoughlin Boulevard (OR Route 99 East), 6 miles south of downtown Portland and .5 mile south of Milwaukie, Oregon. Airplanes were popular additions to gas stations, whether perched atop the roof or "crashed" into it, but few, if any, of these stations are still pumping gas. Opened for business on July 5, 1947, Art Lacey's became an icon for Milwaukie. Lacey opened a drive-in restaurant the next year, but when his twenty-year lease expired, he had to move everything down the road. The station closed in 1991; by then, the plane had suffered the ravages of time and souvenir hunters, but restoration has been under way one piece at a time. Of the 12,731 B-17s built, perhaps fifty remain, an estimated eleven intact. Each "Flying Fortress" is about 74 feet long, 19 feet high, and 103 feet between wingtips. Lacey died in 2000, but his daughter still operates The Bomber restaurant and catering service. The plane's restored nose is displayed at the site in a mini-museum and World War II library called the Wings of Freedom Showcase.
www.thebomber.com

Uncle Sam

Lake George, New York

Uncle Sam guards the entrance to Magic Forest. A Muffler Man turned woodsman tries in vain to hide behind the flagpole. *Photo by Warner Stewart*

ncle Sam, the red, white, and blue clad symbol of the United States, shows up regularly around fireworks tents and car dealers to add a patriotic touch. But there was a real person two centuries ago who likely inspired the symbol.

Samuel Wilson lived in Troy, New York, near Lake George. He packed meat for the U.S. Army during the War of 1812 against Great Britain. He also had his own ships and made his own barrels. The latter were stamped "U.S." for the United States Army, but people joked that the letters meant they came from "Uncle Sam" Wilson. Soon everyone came to associate Uncle Sam with anything from the government.

Artists began drawing the figure with a white beard, tall hat, and red, white, and blue clothes. The most popular image was by artist James Montgomery Flagg, whose *I Want You* painting for the cover of a 1916 *Leslie's Weekly* magazine was adopted for World War I recruitment posters. A decade later, Flagg regaled readers with tales of a cross-county auto trip in *Boulevards All the Way–Maybe*.

STATS

SIZE: 38 feet tall, 4,500 pounds

MADE OF: fiberglass covered with clear coat

BUILT: 1981

Troy has a big statue of Wilson at the corner of River and Third Streets, his grave is there, and the town bills itself as the "Home of Uncle Sam." But another town, Merriam, Indiana, likewise claims that the Samuel Wilson buried in its Chapel Cemetery was the inspiration for the Uncle Sam image.

Taking a lighter approach is Magic Forest, about fifty miles north of Troy, New York. The park has a 38-foot-tall Uncle Sam that was made for the 1981 Connecticut state fair, then brought to Lake George the following year. A sign says it's the world's tallest, though Ottawa Lake, Michigan, boasts of a 42-foot-tall Uncle Sam in the midst of fireworks (and Uncle Sam) alley.

Magic Forest opened in 1963 to catch tourists heading to the Adirondack Mountains. The park has twenty-five rides, animals, and even a horse that dives into water. Fans of roadside giants are in for more treats: Not far from Sam is a giant Santa Claus, and lining the park's wooded trails are dozens of fairy-tale figures come to (fiberglass) life, along with Smokey the Bear, a couple astronauts, and four Muffler Men: Paul Bunyan, Pecos Bill, a clown, and a "half-wit" dressed like an Amish woodsman. Even the park's "greeter guy," dressed in a Magic Forest staff shirt, is giant.

Owner Jack Gillette really likes fiberglass figures, says park representative Shelley Cummins. "There are hundreds of them in the park. Uncle Sam is out front because he is so large that he makes a good landmark for people to find the park."

If you visit . . .

Lake George is both a lake and a town in eastern New York state. Magic Forest is 1 mile south of the town on NY Route 9N, just off I-87 Exit 21.

www.magicforestpark.com

If you like Uncle Sam, you'll also like . . .

- The **fiberglass Uncle Sam** on a platform at All-American Novelties, 6263 Sterns Road, U.S. Route 23 Exit 1, Ottawa Lake, 70 miles southwest of Detroit. There is a virtual fireworks alley along U.S. Route 23, after passing from Ohio into Michigan. A couple other businesses here have inflatable Uncle Sams. The owners of the fiberglass Sam bought him in 1988 from a septic tank dealer, where his black paint job led many to think he was Abe Lincoln. They repainted him, and a couple days before July 4, 2001, he was freshened up with 25 gallons of red, white, and blue as part of Hampton Inns' Save-A-Landmark Program.

- The proud-and-happy looking **Uncle Sam** standing at Eastgate Mall on Shadeland near U.S. Route 40 in Indianapolis, Indiana.

Wigwam Village No. 2
Cave City, Kentucky

F rank Redford grew up in the early 1900s around Horse Cave, Kentucky, an area best known today for Mammoth Cave National Park. On a trip to California in the 1930s, he was impressed by a tepee-shaped building in Long Beach. This likely was the TeePee Barbecue, East Second Street at Fifty-second Place, demolished in 1950. Over the next two decades, Redford built conical tepees that looked nearly identical to the Long Beach lunch stand, with rolled-back flaps, diamond-shaped windows, a zigzag flourish at midpoint, poles sticking out the top, and even a painted swastika, an American Indian motif long before its adoption by Nazis, at which point they were painted over. On each side of the Long Beach lunch stand were small tepee-shaped restrooms, which Redford also adopted.

Upon his return to Kentucky, he first opened a tepee-shaped ice cream stand, about which little is known. Then in 1933, Redford built a gas station on U.S. Route 31E in Horse Cave. Inside a 60-foot-tall stucco tepee was an office and

STATS

SIZE: rooms 30 feet high, office 52 feet high

MADE OF: concrete on steel frames

BUILT: 1937

lunch stand. Two years later, Redford added the twin restrooms and six matching 30-foot-tall cabins. He formed the concrete surfaces to look like hides stretched over poles on the exterior and furnished the interiors with knotty pine paneling along with Indian rugs and blankets. The tepees were arranged around a communal grassy area at a time when many travelers still looked forward to evenings swapping the day's driving adventures. Workers at times wore Indian-style clothing, and Native Americans were sometimes employed as performers. The image the site projected, though in no way representing authentic Indian life, was sufficient to snare tourists visiting the cave region.

The main building at Kentucky's Wigwam Village no longer has a lunchroom but still serves as the office and gift shop. On this September day, it was getting a fresh coat of paint.

Redford applied for a patent for his exterior design in December 1935 and received number D98,617 just two months later. In 1937, he opened a second, larger location in nearby Cave City on U.S. Route 31W, the Dixie Highway. Fifteen tepees again formed a half circle around a taller central tepee office and lunchroom, with a gift shop downstairs.

Ivan Jahn has been operating the Cave City location since 1996. The cabins' knotty pine paneling has been painted over, but the many-sided walls still defy right angles and make the shower an especially interesting shape. The original beds and chairs are made of hickory branches. The bathrooms retain their striking original tilework, but modern travelers will also find color TV and air-conditioning.

It was not until 1939 that Redford decided to expand his chain to other operators. He supplied the plans, which were crucial to builders unfamiliar with the techniques needed, and in return, he was to get one-half of 1 percent of the total profits. High standards of propriety and cleanliness were part of the agreement. Five more villages would open, but only one more (number 7) by Redford himself:

1	Horse Cave, Kentucky	1933–35	6 cabins	demolished 1981
2	Cave City, Kentucky	1937	15 cabins	open
3	New Orleans, Louisiana	1940	3 cabins	closed 1954, demolished
4	Orlando, Florida	1948	27 cabins	demolished 1974
5	Birmingham, Alabama	1940	15 cabins	closed 1964, demolished
6	Holbrook, Arizona	1950	15 cabins	closed 1974, reopened
7	San Bernardino, California	1947	19 cabins	open

This 1940s matchbook shows the standard Wigwam Village layout of cabins around a grassy area, with an office at front and center.

The irregular chronology relative to numbering likely resulted from two other locations that were considered but never built: Luray, Virginia, c. 1939, and Portland, Oregon, c. 1946.

Other tepee-shaped businesses followed Redford's and certainly some of them copied his patented idea. Two were said to be the DLD Tepee Motel in Hastings, Nebraska, and the Wigwam Lodge in Tempe, Arizona. But they were only doing what Redford had done: copying a concept that looked attractive and profitable.

If you visit . . .

Wigwam Village is north of Cave City at 601 North Dixie Highway (U.S. Route 31W). It was listed in the National Register of Historic Places about 1990. The area has other vintage motels, some with neon signs, and attractions such as Guntown Mountain and Dinosaurworld.
www.wigwamvillage.com

If you like Wigwam Village No. 2, you'll also like . . .

• Wigwam Village No. 6, now **Wigwam Motel** on West Hopi Drive (Historic Route 66) in Holbrook, Arizona. It was recently refurbished, though the rooms retain the original tile baths and hickory furniture. It's run by the family of original owner Chester Lewis. He also built a museum here to display his collections of Indian and Civil War artifacts, now expanded to include Route 66 memorabilia. The office tepee was replaced in the 1950s by a service station. The motel closed in 1974, but Lewis's son renovated and reopened it in 1988.
www.cybertrails.com/wigwam

• Wigwam Village No. 7, now lovingly restored as **Wigwam Motel**, just west of San Bernardino at 2728 West Foothill Boulevard (Historic Route 66), Rialto, California. The nearby San Bernardino Route 66 Museum, 1398 North E Street, is on the site of the first McDonald's Restaurant, built in 1948.
www.wigwammotel.com

• **Tepee Curios**, on Route 66, Tucumcari, New Mexico. This 1940s building fronted by half a large tepee offers crafts and souvenirs. It's across from the beloved twelve-unit Blue Swallow Motel (1939), which unfortunately, but we hope temporarily, closed in early 2005.

• **Princess Watahwaso Family Museum**, in a tepee in Old Town, Maine. The structure was originally Chief Poolaw's Tepee, a souvenir stand opened in 1959. It became home to the museum in 2004, named for a popular singer and storyteller of the 1910s and 1920s billed as the "Indian Mezzo-soprano."

• **Mud Creek Hogan**, at 38651 U.S. Route 160, west of Mancos, Colorado. This trading post and craft center opened in 1959. A dozen telephone poles have been turned into a row of giant arrows spread among more normal-size tepees.

At Mud Creek Hogan in Mancos, Colorado, a dozen telephone poles serve as 30-foot-long arrows "shot" among three 25-foot-tall concrete tepees. This was the first roadside attraction restored as part of Hampton Inns' Save-A-Landmark Program. *Photo by Mark Wolfe*

- **The Tee Pee Motel** on Business Route 59 about a mile south of U.S. Route 59 in Wharton, Texas. Opened in 1942, it closed by the 1980s and was used for storing trailers, but new owners plan on restoring the eleven tepees.

- Dozens of wigwam structures, past and present, listed online at **www.dreamscape.com/dbporter/wigwam_nation.htm**

Longaberger's Baskets
Central Ohio

ave Longaberger had a dream: He wanted to build his company's new headquarters in the shape of a basket. "If they can put a man on the moon," he told doubtful bankers and disbelieving accountants, "they can certainly build a building that's shaped like a basket."

It's hard to be a dreamer, a visionary, but here was a man who should have been taken seriously. Despite having epilepsy and a stutter that made him dif-

STATS	Picnic Basket	Home Office	Apple Basket
SIZE:	23 feet high	160 feet tall + handles	29 feet tall
MADE OF:	hardwood maple	cement and stucco	hardwood maple
BUILT:	1980	1997	1999

ficult to understand, Dave Longaberger was a hard worker who treated people well. His father was a basketmaker; Dave loved watching him craft baskets in the workshop behind their house. Years later, after going through a string of jobs, Dave noticed that stores were beginning to sell imported baskets and wondered if there might yet be a market for the tight, handwoven kind his father used to make. In 1973, he founded The Longaberger Company. His baskets cost at least double the imported ones, but Dave believed a superior product would find its place in the market. Fine craftsmanship and in-home demonstrations helped the company become the largest maker of handmade baskets in the United States, not to mention the leading owner of giant baskets.

The Longaberger Home Office building in Newark, Ohio, puts to rest which one is *really* the largest basket.

The first was built in 1980 as the World's Largest Picnic Basket in Dave's hometown of Dresden, Ohio; it's 19 feet wide, 48 feet long, and 23 feet high. The "Picnic" part has been dropped from its title, and it was rewoven in 2001 by company workers who took the old wood off and replaced it with wood from ten hardwood maple trees. Just down Main Street is a soda shop once owned by Dave and given his nickname, Popeye's.

The headquarters, or Home Office, is not a real basket; it's covered in stucco. But the seven-story building is shaped exactly like the company's Medium Market Basket, just 160 times larger. Cherry woodwork came from Longaberger property in Hanover and was milled, shaped, and finished by company craftspeople. On top are handles weighing 75 tons each. They're heated in winter to prevent ice from forming. Tours are offered daily, and nearby is the factory where workers

The World's Largest Basket, in Dresden, Ohio.

The World's Largest Apple Basket, at the Longaberger Homestead in Frazeysburg, Ohio. *The Longaberger Company*

LONGABERGER'S BASKETS **71**

make up to forty-five thousand baskets every day. Longaberger's Home Office is trademarked, which is rare for a building.

Rounding out the trio of sites is the Longaberger Homestead, a shopping and dining attraction where visitors can even weave their own baskets. It's also home to the World's Largest Apple Basket, 19 feet in diameter at its base and 29 feet tall if you count the handle.

Dave died in 1999, but his daughter Rachel heads the philanthropic Longaberger Foundation, and daughter Tami oversees fifty-four hundred employees and seventy thousand independent home consultants as CEO of the Longaberger Company. The business now sells a variety of products but still makes baskets by hand, just as Dave's father once did.

If you visit . . .

The Home Office is at 1500 East Main Street (parallel to OH Route 16) in Newark, about 35 miles east of Columbus.
www.longaberger.com

The Longaberger Homestead, with the Apple Basket, is in Frazeysburg, 17 miles east of the Home Office on OH Route 16.
www.zanesville-ohio.com/longaberger_homestead.htm

Dresden is another 8 miles east; the big basket is at Fifth and Main Streets.
www.basketvillageusa.com

If you like the Longaberger Baskets, you'll also like . . .

- **The Kegs**, with two orange-red, 20-foot-high root beer barrels, built in 1934, flanking a classic drive-in restaurant at 901 North Fifth Street, Grand Forks, North Dakota. If they look like the big keg seen in old postcards for Bill Wood's Triple XXX Famous Foods drive-in of Waco, Texas, that's because this was a franchise location, albeit a distant one. The second keg was brought here when the original franchisee closed another location.

- The big **apple** in front of Kimberly's Gift Boutique, 135 North Braddock Street (U.S. Route 11) in Winchester, Virginia. The apple was built to celebrate the apple-growing industry in the state's northern reaches. The town also holds an Apple Blossom Festival the first weekend in May. Winchester is on I-81; U.S. Routes 11 and 50 meet just south of the apple.

Plain Folk
Southeastern Pennsylvania

ROADSIDE AMERICA
Shartlesville PA.

n southeastern Pennsylvania, it seems that every restaurant advertises Pennsylvania Dutch cooking. Well, maybe not all of them, but more than a few feature hog maw (pig stomach stuffed with sausage, potatoes, and onions), or *schnitz un gnepp* (ham with apple and dumplings), or scrapple (fried slices of a pork-based gruel thickened with buckwheat flour and cornmeal). Even mainstream restaurants hang hex signs or paint ornate hearts, tulips, and distelfinks, hoping to capture some of the goodwill people feel toward the "plain people."

The Pennsylvania Dutch first left Europe's Rhine River valley in the seventeenth century, mostly to escape religious persecution but also to take advantage of the fertile lands in Pennsylvania. "Dutch," derived from the German word *Deutsch*, does not refer to people from the Netherlands in this case, but to the German-speaking emigrants from the Palatinate, Wurttemberg, Baden, Alsace, and Switzerland. While the majority were Lutheran and Reformed, a small percentage were Anabaptist–Amish, Mennonites, and other small groups. People from these sects, particularly the Amish, have remained much the same through the years and are called plain because their clothes are simple. Mostly farmers, many do not use cars or electricity. Even the prevalent hex signs of the region are not displayed on the barns of the Amish, Mennonites, and the more strict sects of the Pennsylvania Dutch. So it is ironic that photos, dolls, and giant statues of the plain people are used to advertise tourist businesses. It is a cottage industry gone big-time, and the predilection of the plain folk for shunning modern conveniences is exactly what brings more people to see them.

An Amish couple at Road-side America in Shartlesville, Pennsylvania, draws travelers off U.S. Route 22. Photo by Shari DeSalvo-Paglia

At Roadside America in Shartlesville, an Amish couple is frozen in a wave greeting those arriving at the "World's Greatest Indoor Miniature Village." Opened in 1953, when U.S. Route 22 was relocated, the attraction has more than three hundred miniature buildings and four thousand tiny people, unchanged in the four decades since founder Laurence Gieringer passed away. The waving folks were built by Rodman Shutt of Strasburg, creator of numerous fiberglass giants that made their way beyond the region.

The Holiday Inn north of Lancaster also has a larger-than-life Amish couple. Local craftsman Irvin A. Lichty created them in 1972 to attract travelers on the new U.S. Route 30 bypass. Hotel general manager Karen Cristina says many of their guests take pictures with "Mom and Pop," and the couple even have their own Cat's Meow collectible. Cristina says the display needs some work, however: "The upkeep has generally been cleaning and paint touchup semiannually, but this year the hex sign between the couple has deteriorated. The plywood has rotted, and the estimated cost of repairs to just the sign is $15,000. If we are unable to come up with the money for repairs, we will be forced to remove this part of the structure."

A giant woman holding a pie outside Granny's Restaurant in Frackville is accompanied by a little girl holding a doll, which has been missing its head for as long as anyone can recall. They were made by a local craftsman for Hamburg's Pot-o-Gold Diner, a Swingle-brand diner that sat astride U.S. Route 22 at the PA Route 61 interchange. When the manufacturer repossessed the diner in the 1980s, the statues were moved to Granny's, which opened in 1986.

Perhaps the best-known regional giant is Amos, an Amish farmer that watched over Zinn's Diner in nearby Denver. Christian Zinn opened the diner in 1950 and added Amos in 1960. He was made to look like Christian but was named for the father of the family baby-sitter. When the diner was remodeled in 1969, with the stainless exterior covered by pebble-textured walls, a sturdier, better-proportioned Amos was built by local fiberglass craftsman Rod Shutt. The

STATS	Roadside America	Holiday Inn	Granny's	Hershey
SIZE:	approx. 10 feet	11 feet	15 feet	15 feet
MADE OF:	fiberglass	fiberglass	stucco	fiberglass
BUILT:	c. 1960	1972	c. 1975	1969

Another Amish couple greets visitors passing the Holiday Inn on U.S. Route 30 north of Lancaster. *Photo by Kyle Weaver*

new Amos held a rake and talked when visitors pushed a button, regaling them with Amish wisdom and reminding them to try some shoo-fly pie.

Why the past tense? When the Zinn family sold the diner in 2003, Amos had to move. Grandson Chris Zinn donated the 300-pound statue to the Lancaster Trust. Staff at its Heritage Center Museum cleaned the giant and repaired the corroded support structure. Trouble is, it's hard to find space for a two-story-tall farmer. In September 2004, he was sent on a five-year loan to the Hershey Farm Restaurant, southeast of Lancaster in Strasburg, where you'll find him wearing a newly painted purple shirt but no longer talking.

If you visit . . .

The Amish couple at Roadside America guard the parking lot between the main building and the Pennsylvania Dutch Gift Haus. I-78 (U.S. Route 22) runs in front but has no direct access; take Exit 23, Shartlesville.

   www.roadsideamericainc.com

The Amish couple at the Holiday Inn is north of Lancaster, Pennsylvania, on U.S. Route 30, Greenfield Road exit, next to the Pennsylvania Dutch Convention and Visitor's Bureau.

   www.holiday-inn.com/ins-visitors

Granny's Restaurant and its pie woman are at 115 West Coal Street (PA Route 61), just north of Frackville. She can also be seen from I-81.

   www.grannys-pa.com

A Pennsylvania Dutch mother and child attract drivers off I-81 to Granny's Restaurant on PA Route 61, just north of Frackville.
Photo by Kyle Weaver

Amos is at the Hershey Farm Restaurant and Inn, 240 Hartman Bridge Road (PA Route 896), east of Lancaster and 1.5 miles south of U.S. Route 30. The site's 23 acres also include a motel, general store, fishing pond, vegetable gardens, petting farm, and play area, and adjoin the Sight & Sound Millennium Theatre. **www.hersheyfarm.com**

If you like Plain Folk, you'll also like . . .

• The big **Amish boy** at the Freeze and Frizz restaurant, down the road from the new home of Amos at 200 Hartman Bridge Road (PA Route 896) in Strasburg. He holds an ice cream cone in one hand and a burger-eating piglet in the other, and a banana split-eating daddy pig sits in a wheelbarrow. A fishing pole has inspired locals to name him Huckleberry Finn. The set was crafted by Rod Shutt about 1976.

• The 20-foot-tall fiberglass **Amish Man** at Shirey's Auto Sales at 2000 South Bay Road (U.S. Route 113/ DE Route 1), just north of Milford, Delaware. He originated as a mascot when the Reading, Pennsylvania-based Dempsey's Diner chain bought the M&M Diner in New Castle, Delaware, to advertise the company's Pennsylvania Dutch-style cooking. When the chain started using chubby Dutch boys, the 12-foot-tall man was sold to the Country Pantry, another Pennsylvania Dutch-themed place on U.S. Route 13 in Dover, Delaware, then settled at Shirey's in 2000.

Amos welcomed visitors to Zinn's Diner until the restaurant changed hands in 2003.

Westward Ho
Covered Wagon
Milford, Nebraska

The Covered Wagon once had a giant cowboy: gone. It had other themed attractions: closed. It had four big wheels: missing. At least the wagon body survives.

Ken Dahle wanted to build a monument to the pioneers. About 1970, he brought a one-room schoolhouse and old-time church here astride the newly opened I-80. He added a museum, gift shop, motel, and campground, with restrooms in a big wood-covered tepee, and another nearby. By 1976, Dahle was pumping Phillips 66 gas at his larger-than-life wagon. It originally had at least one side splayed outward, which was a trait of Conestoga wagons, helping the loads settle back toward the center. An adjacent Muffler Man got a big red Stetson and became a cowboy. Dahle called his collection Westward Ho.

Dahle's 66 I-80 Service thrived, and he had plans to add giant oxen to the wagon, but consumers increasingly looked for big chain stations. Then Dahle died, and by the late 1990s, the pumps were gone. In 2001, the cowboy was sent west, settling at G's Cowboy Shop on U.S. Route 14 just west of Cody, Wyoming. The 23-foot-diameter wheels were likewise removed. All that's left of the station is the wagon, now housing a motorcycle shop. The other Westward Ho buildings remain, but they sit, slowly decaying, in tall grass. Today pioneers are honored with a modern-day giant: the Great Platte River Road Arch, which spans all four lanes of I-80, 50 miles to the west near Kearney, Nebraska.

The covered wagon may never finish its trip west now that it's lost its wheels.

STATS

SIZE: 50 feet high, 48 feet long, 30 feet wide

MADE OF: block building, curved wood-frame roof, asphalt shingles

BUILT: 1972–76

If you visit . . .

The Covered Wagon, now Outlaw Cycle, is about 15 miles west of Lincoln, Nebraska, on I-80, Exit 382, at 965 238th Street.
www.milford-ne.com/businesses/auto/outlaw_cycle.html

If you like the Covered Wagon, you'll also like . . .

- The **pair of oxen pulling a wagon** at The Covered Wagon, a closed souvenir shop 5 miles west of Kearney, Nebraska, on the Lincoln Highway (U.S. Route 30).

- Two **big buffalo**, symbols of the Old West. One made of 4½ miles of barbed wire can be found at the Sod House Museum in Gothenburg, Nebraska, at I-80, just north of Exit 211. The other, a 26-foot-tall cement buffalo, is at Frontier Village in Jamestown, North Dakota, near the intersection of I-94 Exit 258 and U.S. Route 281.
www.websteader.com/wbstdsodmuzm.htm
www.buffalomuseum.com/frontier/htm

- The 36-foot-tall **prospector** Last Chance Joe at Nugget Casino, 1100 Nugget Avenue (but at the Victorian Street entrance), Sparks, Nevada. Joe has greeted visitors to the casino since the 1950s.
www.janugget.com

Twistee Treat
Ice Cream Cones
Lots of locations

ot every Programatic building is old. The Twistee Treat chain began making its ice cream cone stands in 1983. They look like a wide soft-serve, cake cone, most with a cherry on top. About two dozen were built in Florida before the company closed around 1990. Those, and others around the country, are now independently operated, leading to offerings like ice cream and gourmet coffee. As the cones are remodeled and sometimes converted to other uses, they increasingly differ from each other. The cone building in Kissimmee, Florida, is topped with rainbow sprinkles. The ice cream on the cone in Port Charlotte, Florida, is pink.

STATS
SIZE: 22 feet tall, 20 feet wide
MADE OF: fiberglass
BUILT: 1983 to present

Information on the company and its cones is tough to pin down; Twistee Treat Canada remains but does not oversee the U.S. locations. Its flagship store, operated by the company itself, is at 1752 Dundas Street, East London, Ontario.

A nice Twistee Treat at 2629 Lincoln Way west in Massillon, Ohio.

About thirty cone buildings survive, mostly on the East Coast and most still using the Twistee Treat name. The cone is usually yellow with white topping, but it seems an alternate style had ice cream with a chocolate-vanilla swirl. The Canadian company has standardized its ten or so cones, with the toppings striped in colors to advertise the thirty soft-serve flavors that are rotated throughout the year.

Surprisingly, few ice cream shops have tried to emulate an entire cone. The Kone Inn, built seven decades ago in Eagle Rock, California, had a cone on each corner of a square building. The Big Cone chain in Southern California used an upside-down sugar cone that looked more like a tepee. Hand-cranked ice cream freezers were more common, along with hand-packed containers, such as the famous Freda Farms cartons, all now out of fashion.

If you visit . . .

Twistee Treat cone-shaped buildings were located in the following towns, though business names may have changed, shops may have closed, or the buildings may have been moved.

Florida: Boca Raton, Bonita Springs, Clermont, Dade City, Englewood, Eustis, Fort Myers (U.S. Route 41), Hudson, Jacksonville, Kenneth City, Kissimmee, Lakeland (two), New Port Richey (two), North Fort Myers (the chain's first), Ocoee, Okeechobee, Orlando (two), Palatka, Panama City, Plant City, Pompano Beach, Port Charlotte, Port St. Lucie, Rotunda West, Saint Augustine, Sarasota, Seminole, St. Petersburg Beach (two), Stuart, Tampa (two), Tavares, Winter Park, Zephyrhills.

Illinois: East Peoria.

Kansas: Great Bend, Oakley.

Michigan: Perry.

Missouri: Kansas City, Knob Noster.

New York: Batavia, Niagara Falls.

Ohio: Canton, Clyde, Massillon (four), Strasburg.

Pennsylvania: Bristol, Philadelphia.

This sign alerts all to Kennywood Park's beloved square Dip Cones in West Mifflin, Pennsylvania.

For more on Twistee Treat Canada, visit **www.twisteetreat.net**

If you like Twistee Treat stands, you'll also like . . .

- The few Twistee Treat cone buildings that survive with new names: **Twist o' the Mist**, 18 Niagara Street, Niagara Falls, New York; **Dave's Treats**, 36305 State Road 54, Zephyrhills, Florida.

- **The Dairy Dome** (now closed) in Panama City, Florida, a home-built cone with soft serve on top. The wide base is not as well proportioned as the Twistee Treat versions and looks more like a barrel.

- **The Sundae** on Business U.S. Route 30 East in Everett, Pennsylvania, shaped like a big scoop of ice cream.

- **Milk bottles** that were used to market daisy products. Bottles, mostly stucco, are found across the country, many concentrated in Massachusetts. The **Quonquont Dairy Milk Bottle** in Whately has been restored and moved to outside the municipal and historical society offices on Chestnut Plain Road. Milk bottles built by the **Frates Dairy**, c. 1930, survive in Raynham, New Bedford, and Boston, and still serve as food outlets (the Boston location, which later served Hood Dairy, is ringed with distinctive windows with awnings). You can live inside one of three milk bottles at the former **Richland Dairy**, now incorporated into the 113-unit Richmond Dairy Apartments, 201 W Marshall Street, a block north of Broad Street in Richmond, Virginia. Washington state also has a number of bottles, including the two built c. 1935 by **Benewah Dairy** at 802 W. Garland Street (now Mary Lou's Milk Bottle) and 321 S. Cedar Street.

Dinosaur Park

Rapid City, South Dakota

Brontosaurus (or Apatosaurus), tallest of all at Dinosaur Park, overlooking Rapid City, South Dakota. *Photo by Beth Boland*

When the carving of Mount Rushmore commenced in 1927, tourists began streaming to the southwest corner of South Dakota. Nearby businesses saw gold; not the kind Lt. Col. George Custer had discovered in these Black Hills half a century earlier, but in the form of tourist dollars. Roadside attractions sprang up and continue to surround the monument and the roads leading to it.

About 75 miles to the east are the Badlands, filled with spectacular weathered rocks and rich with dinosaur fossils. One of the stops on the Milwaukee Railroad was the tiny town of Creston, also along SD Route 44. The owners of the Creston General Store thought a dinosaur statue might draw some customers, so in 1933, they built a 25-foot-long concrete dino across the road.

Rapid City, only 20 miles from Mount Rushmore, also longed for more tourists, especially in the midst of the Depression. Town leaders wanted a sculpture at the north end of winding Skyline Drive, a federal relief project started in 1934. A local paleontologist suggested full-size dinosaur statues; they were soon under way with help from the Works Progress Administration, making this among the most peculiar of public works projects.

Dinosaur Park, towering over the city from the west, was dedicated on May 22, 1936, though it took two more years to complete. Originally there were five concrete dinosaurs: Brontosaurus, the tall one; Stegosaurus, with ridged bumps on the back; Trachodon, with a duck bill, now called Anototitan; Triceratops, with two long horns; and Tyrannosaurus Rex, which seems ready to pounce on Triceratops. They were later joined by two smaller ones: Dimetrodon and Protoceatos. They are made with pipe frames, wire mesh to form the curves, and concrete skin. The Brontosaurus can be seen from far away, especially at night, when it's lit. (Brontosaurus is now called Apatosaurus by paleontologists, but the old, more familiar term helps one envision the long-necked dino.)

The overlook was made an official city park in 1968 and was listed in the National Register of Historic Places in 1990. Private dinosaur parks were much more common and could be found across the country, but only a few carry on. Prehistoric animals now tend to gravitate toward "legitimate" educational attractions.

STATS

SIZES:
Brontosaurus: 80 feet long, 28 feet high
Stegosaurus: 11 feet long, 7 feet high
Trachodon: 33 feet long, 17^1/$_2$ feet high
Triceratops: 27 feet long, 11 feet high
Tyrannosaurus Rex: 35 feet long, 16 feet high

MADE OF: steel skeleton covered with wire mesh and concrete skin

BUILT: 1936–38

If you visit . . .

Dinosaur Park, including a gift shop, is west of downtown Rapid City along Skyline Drive, which is just south of Business I-90 and SD Routes 44 and 79. For more information, contact the Rapid City Convention and Visitors Bureau.
  www.rapidcitycvb.com

You're almost there! A sign for Dinosaurworld in Cave City, Kentucky.

If you like Dinosaur Park, you'll also like . . .

• The nearby **Creston Dinosaur,** 20 feet tall and 60 feet long, made with wind-mill framing, bridge ties, and railroad bolts, northwest of Badlands National Park and the town of Scenic, just north of SD Route 44. It was assembled by the town blacksmith and covered in concrete. The original road was bypassed long ago, and the few buildings are gone. Only a nearby bridge over the Cheyenne River remains, and the dinosaur, which was completely refurbished by civil engineering students from the South Dakota School of Mines and Technology in 1998.

• The **Crazy Horse Memorial,** a giant rock carving like nearby Mount Rushmore. Four miles north of Custer, South Dakota, on U.S. Routes 16/385, the memorial honors the nineteenth-century leader of the Lakota Indians, and when finished, it will be the world's largest statue.

• The 6-foot **jackalope** (a pretend cross between a jackrabbit and an antelope) and the 80-foot-long **Brontosaurus** that overlooks the eastern entrance to Wall Drug, about 50 miles east of Rapid City at Exits 109 and 110 of I-90. Wall Drug is a wacky tourist attraction north of the Badlands in Wall, South Dakota. www.walldrug.com

• **Dinosaur Gardens Prehistoric Zoo** on the western shore of Lake Huron on U.S. Route 23 in Ossineke, Michigan. The zoo has a curious mix of dinos with cavemen and cavewomen, which never coexisted in real life. Founder Paul Domke spent four decades sculpting a couple dozen creatures in an effort to

While visiting Florida's Gulf Coast, have your car serviced inside Harold's 100-foot-long dinosaur. *Photo by Martin Coble*

resolve the theory of evolution with the book of Genesis. Most notable is an 85-foot-long Brontosaurus with a staircase to its belly.

- **Dinosaur Gardens,** at the Cabazon exit of I-10, about 18 miles west of Palm Springs, California. The dinosaurs were created by Claude Bell, who grew up playing near Lucy the Elephant. Inspired to build his own creations, he first made figures for California's Knott's Berry Farm amusement park. He then opened the Wheel Inn restaurant along I-10 and spent years building a 150-foot-long Brontosaurus named Dinney and a 65-foot Tyrannosaurus named Rex on 76 acres of desert land. You can see them in the 1985 Tim Burton movie, *Pee Wee's Big Adventure*.

- **Dinosaur Land** at 3848 Stonewall Jackson Highway (U.S. Route 522) in White Post, Virginia, between Winchester and Front Royal, about 25 miles south of the Maryland border. Visiting this park is like walking through a forest of forty frozen prehistoric animals. It has a great gift shop too. www.dinosaurland.com

- **Dinosaurworld,** similar outdoor museums in Cave City, Kentucky (I-65, Exit 53), and Plant City, Florida (I-4, Exit 17), just east of Tampa. www.dinoworld.net

- **Prehistoric Forest,** at 8232 East Harbor Road (OH Route 163), Marblehead, Ohio, across Sandusky Bay from Cedar Point. This decades-old attraction along Lake Erie in northern Ohio features a tram ride through a forest of dinosaurs. A few move and make sounds, but most of the noise comes from toy machine guns that guests are given to shoot the monsters. The founder also built a Prehistoric Forest in Irish Hills, Michigan. Next door is Mystery Hill, a gravity-defying attraction, and just down the road is a 20-foot-tall cook that once served Jacques roast beef restaurants in Mansfield.

- **Harold's Auto Service,** in a former Sinclair station on U.S. Route 19, Spring Hill, Florida, near Weeki Wachi. You may recall the big brontos that Sinclair placed *next* to its stations in the 1960s. This station *is* a dinosaur, framed in steel and covered with cement.

Shell-Shaped Station
Winston-Salem, North Carolina

An office for historic preservationists is a fitting outcome for this station in Winston-Salem, North Carolina. *Photo by Martin Coble*

Quality Oil was organized in 1929 to be a jobber, or distributor, for Shell Oil. Quality's first location, opened that December in Winston-Salem, was a common brick station with flat roof and canopy. But with the region already dominated by larger oil companies, what better way to promote Shell than to build service stations shaped like big shells? By 1930, concrete was being slathered atop bent wood-and-wire frames, and the first shell-shaped station opened that June. A patent was filed a month later, and two more shells opened that year. Eventually eight were built.

This was at the height of Programatic architecture, and service stations in particular were open to experimentation. Windmills, wigwams, and castles were popular motifs with entrepreneurs; Greek temples, English cottages, Spanish

STATS

SIZE: 16 feet high, 20 feet wide

MADE OF: bent green wood, wire, and concrete

BUILT: probably 1932

missions, and Colonial stations were favored by corporations. The 3-D representations of Shell Oil's trademark served as both oversize signs and local landmarks.

The public embraced the eight shell-shaped stations, which positioned Quality as a forward-thinking company, but the outlets were too small to generate much profit. The last one was built in 1933. Shell Oil built a much larger shell-shaped information booth at the 1935 California Pacific International Exhibition in San Diego, but by then its stations were conventional and included indoor bays.

Quality Oil expanded through the years and continues to operate minimarts and other businesses in North and South Carolina and Virginia. The company considered restoring one of the shells but never carried through with the idea. About 1964, Quality closed the lone survivor, number seven of the eight built, and it then housed other businesses, longest as a small engine repair shop. In 1975, it became the first service station to be listed in the National Register of Historic Places.

Preservation North Carolina (PNC), based in Raleigh, became part owner with the idea of not only restoring the building, but also establishing a satellite office inside. Founded in 1939, PNC is the state's only private, nonprofit preservation organization, and it operates without state or federal support. The group has saved almost five hundred endangered historic properties by acquiring them and then finding buyers who can rehabilitate them.

Funding had to be obtained from a variety of sources, including the North Carolina Department of Cultural Resources and a restoration grant from Shell Oil Company. Restoration began in September 1996.

Workers chipped off layers of faded paint to discover the original yellow-orange color beneath. They fixed a crack that had been patched with tar and rebuilt a trellis that had provided shade when attendants washed and lubricated cars. Quality Oil donated restored gas pumps and pole lamps with attractive shell-shaped globes. The interior of the Shell was remade into an office, which has shelves lined with old photos of the station. It took seven months and $55,000 to restore, but today one of the premier restorations of a roadside giant is home to the preservation agency that spearheaded the effort.

If you visit . . .

The Shell houses the PNC Northwest Office at 1111 Sprague Street at Peachtree Street, Winston-Salem, North Carolina.
www.presnc.org/seerestorations/shellstation/shellstation.html

If you like the Shell Station, you'll also like . . .

- **The Teapot Dome Station** in south-central Washington, perhaps the only roadside attraction named for a presidential scandal. In 1921, President Warren G. Harding's secretary of the interior gave lease rights for U.S. Navy oil reserves

The Beautiful GULF LIGHTHOUSE SERVICE STATION County Causeway . . . Miami Beach, Florida

Lighthouses, like the one on this 1937 postcard, remain a popular motif for those long the shore, or those who wish they were.

in Teapot Dome, Wyoming, to private interests, hence the Teapot Dome scandal. The red and white teapot-shaped station was built near Granger the next year to poke fun at the troubles. It was moved about a mile in 1928, and then with the arrival of I-82 half a century later, it was moved a couple more miles to its current location. During the second move, the station was hit by a car and ended up sitting vacant for years. It was restored in 1984 and earned a spot in the National Register of Historic Places. The teapot—13 feet high and 15 feet in diameter—closed in March 2004 as a result of vandalism, rising gas prices, and slow business, but the site is still well kept. The station is accessible from I-82, Exit 54, at 14691 Yakima Valley Highway (U.S. Route 12), a mile southeast of Zillah, Washington, and about 15 miles southeast of Yakima.

• **The World's Largest Gas Pump**, built in the 1930s as the office for a service station in Maryville, Missouri. The metal-covered, wood-frame building has since been moved to a city park in King City, Missouri, with similar streamlined electric gas pumps out front.

FURTHER READING AND SURFING

Books

Andrews, J.C.C. *The Well-Built Elephant and Other Roadside Attractions: A Tribute to American Eccentricity*. New York: Congdon and Weed, 1984.

Arbogast, Joan Marie. *Buildings in Disguise: Architecture That Looks like Animals, Food, and Other Things*. Honesdale, Pa.: Boyds Mills Press, 2004.

Baeder, John. *Gas, Food, and Lodging: A Postcard Odyssey, Through the Great American Roadside*. New York: Abbeville Press, 1982.

Barth, Jack, Doug Kirby, Ken Smith, and Mike Wilkins. *Roadside America*. New York: Fireside, 1986.

Bergheim, Laura A. *Weird Wonderful America*. New York: Tilden Press, 1988.

Blake, Peter. *God's Own Junkyard: The Planned Deterioration of America's Landscape*. New York: Holt, Rinehart and Winston, 1964.

Friedman, Jan. *Eccentric America*. Buck, England: Bradt Travel Guides, 2001.

Genovese, Peter. *Roadside New Jersey*. New Brunswick, N.J.: Rutgers University Press, 1994.

Heimann, Jim. *California Crazy and Beyond: Roadside Vernacular Architecture*. San Francisco: Chronicle Books, 2001.

Heimann, Jim, and Rip Georges. *California Crazy: Roadside Vernacular Architecture*. San Francisco: Chronicle Books, 1980.

Jakle, John A., and Keith A. Sculle. *The Gas Station in America*. Baltimore: Johns Hopkins University Press, 1994.

Jennings, Jan ed. *Roadside America: The Automobile in Design and Culture*. Ames: Iowa State University Press for the Society for Commercial Archeology, 1990.

Kirby, Doug, Ken Smith, and Mike Wilkins. *The New Roadside America*. New York: Fireside, 1992.

Liebs, Chester H. *Main Street to Miracle Mile: American Roadside Architecture*. Baltimore: Johns Hopkins University Press, 1985.

Margolies, John. *The End of the Road: Vanishing Highway Architecture in America*. New York: Penguin Books, 1981.

——. *Fun along the Road: American Tourist Attractions*. Boston: Bullfinch, 1998.

Margolies, John, and Emily Gwathmey, *Signs of Our Time*. New York: Abbeville Press, 1993.

Marling, Karal Ann. *The Colossus of Roads: Myth and Symbol along the American Highway*. Minneapolis: University of Minnesota Press, 1984.

Pohlen, Jerome. *Oddball Florida: A Guide to Some Really Strange Places*. Chicago: Chicago Review Press, 2004. See also his other books: *Oddball Indiana*, 2002; *Oddball Illinois*, 2000; and *Oddball Wisconsin*, 2001.

Venturi, Robert, Denise Scott Brown, and Steven Izenour. *Learning from Las Vegas: The Forgotten Symbolism of Architectural Form*. Cambridge, Mass.: MIT Press, 1977. Revised version of 1972 edition.

Zurcher, Neil. *Ohio Oddities*. Cleveland: Gray & Company, 2001.

Websites

www.agilitynut.com/roadside.html
Great pictures and captions from traveler Debra Jane Seltzer.

www.bigthings.ca
Canadian giants.

www.cr.nps.gov/nr/twhp/wwwlps/lcssons/6roadside/6roadside.htm
Teaching with Historic Places—Roadside Attractions is a classroom-ready lesson plan that examines seven examples of roadside architecture, some giant.

www.fastkorp.com
FAST Corporation is the leading maker of fiberglass statues.

www.jimsbigthings.com
Lots of great pictures showing Jim Hejl in relation to big things.

www.roadsideamerica.com
The most comprehensive roadside attractions site from the authors of *Roadside America*.

www.roadsideattractions.ca
More Canadian giants.

www.sca-roadside.org
Since 1975, the Society for Commercial Archeology's print publications—the *News, Journal*, and *NewsJournal*—have reported on the roadside, including giants, and the evolving awareness and historiography of the field. The spring–summer 1995 *Journal* was devoted to Programatic architecture.

www.signmuseum.org
The not-for-profit American Sign Museum is five minutes from downtown Cincinnati at 2515 Essex Avenue in the Essex Studios building, Walnut Hills. More than 200 signs are on display. Its archives of books, catalogs, and photos are held at the business office at ST Media Group, 407 Gilbert Avenue, Cincinnati.

www.wlra.us
World's Largest Roadside Attractions in the United States and Canada.

www.worldslargestdoc.com
Pictures and stories from the making of *World's Largest*, a one-hour documentary that profiles the towns and people behind some of the country's "world's largest" attractions and what they mean to their often-rural communities.

www.worldslargestthings.com
The World's Largest Collection of the World's Smallest Versions of the World's Largest Things. Artist Erika Nelson travels in her customized bus filled with miniature replicas of roadside giants.

ACKNOWLEDGMENTS

ditor Kyle Weaver has once again managed to graciously marshal another project, which means much more than just editing the words; you'll find his handiwork throughout and even some of his photographs. Supporting his work on the book were copyeditor Joyce Bond, managing editor Amy Cooper, paginator Kerry Handel, sales director Patrick Moran, designer Beth Oberholtzer, specialty accounts manager Donna Pope, advertising art director Wendy Reynolds, art director Caroline Stover, and many others at Stackpole Books.

Lots of others have helped through the years, including JoAnn Adams; Carol Ahlgren; John Axtell and Diana Ames; Shannon Jackson Arnold; Michael A. Bedeau, Comstock Historic District Commission; Charles Biddle and Eileen O'Hare; Beth Boland, National Register of Historic Places; Gerald and Carol Bomba; Frank Brusca; Kevin and Lori Butko; Diane Campbell, Dallas Zoo; Martha Carver, Tennessee Department of Transportation; Jim Cassler; Martin Coble; Jim Conkle; Steve Cotham, Knox County Public Library System; Karen Cristina, Holiday Inn Visitors Center; Thom Crosby, Pal's Sudden Service; Shelley Cummins, Magic Forest; Shari DeSalvo-Paglia; Andrew Evans, Twistee Treat Canada; Michael Eversmeyer; Tim Ezzell, University of Tennessee; Chris Faivre, Las Cruces CVB; Mike Gassmann and Judy DeMoisy, Downtown Collinsville Inc.; Peter Genovese; Timothy C. Glines, Minnesota Historical Society; Cindy Habedank and Gayle Quistgard, Bemidji Visitors & Convention Bureau; Rich Helfant, Lucy the Elephant; Olga Herbert, Karen Fetter, and Kristin Poerschke, Lincoln Highway Heritage Corridor; Jim Heimann; Daniel Hershberger, University of Michigan Transportation Institute; Carol Ingald; Angie Jordan and Jeff Whetzel, Longaberger; Rachel Kennedy; Brian Kutchak; Sara Amy Leach; Jennifer Lehto; Joann Leight, Dinosaur Land; John Margolies; Karal Ann Marling; Douglas McCombs; John Milan; Mary Beth Miller; Chris B. Nelson, South Dakota Historical Society; Julie Nelson, Camp Snoopy, Mall of America; Russell Rein; Beth Savage, National Register of Historic Places; Kelly Saville, Illinois State Historic Preservation Agency; Carrie Scupholm; Rick Sebak, WQED-TV; Cory Seeman; Debra Jane Seltzer; Claudette Stager, Tennessee Historical Commission; Warner Stewart; Tod Swormstedt, American Sign Museum; Douglas Towne; Michael Wallis; Larry Weintraub, Randy's Donuts; Margaret Westfield, Westfield Architects and Preservation Consultants; Mark Wolfe; Don Yoder.